Faith, Family, and Memories

Faith, Family, and Memories

Stories of Our Journey through Life
in the United States, Mexico, and Back

Sue W. Sanchez

ISBN (paperback): 978-1-965211-00-7
ISBN (ebook): 978-1-965211-01-4

Book design and production by www.AuthorSuccess.com
Front cover by www.adobestock.com

Printed in the United States of America

Contents

Prologue: My Three Lives   ix

PART 1: MY FIRST LIFE: 1
Growing Up in the United States: Nineteen Years (1951-1969)

    Chapter One: When? Where? To Whom?   3
    Chapter Two: Two Amazing People, Blessings from God   9

PART 2: MY SECOND LIFE: 19
Life in Mexico (Mexico City, Oaxaca, Tuxtla Gutierrez,
and Tapachula): 22 Years (1970-1992)

    Chapter Three: A New Door Opened   21
    Chapter Four: A Piano Before a Stove   28
    Chapter Five: Our Perfect Place   33
    Chapter Six: Surprise! Here's Our New Baby!   37
    Chapter Seven: We Didn't See These Things Coming!   40
    Chapter Eight: Yikes! What just happened?   46
         or The Birth of Our Second Daughter
    Chapter Nine: Baby Number Three   49
    Chapter Ten: Education in Tuxtla   52
    Chapter Eleven: Times to Pray and Times to Play   57
         Family Traditions and Celebrations   66
    Chapter Twelve: What's a Rosca de Reyes?   67
    Chapter Thirteen: Halloween   70
    Chapter Fourteen: The Día de los Muertos   75
         The Day of the Dead
    Chapter Fifteen: Watch Out! You're Going to Get Stoned!   81
    Chapter Sixteen: Earthquakes and Volcanos   86

Chapter Seventeen: Good-bye, My Dear Friend!   89
Until We Meet Again!

Chapter Eighteen: The Pope Is Coming!   92

Chapter Nineteen: The Rise and Fall of My Earthly Rock   95

PART THREE: MY THIRD LIFE: 101
Back to the United States (El Paso): 1992 Until Now

Chapter Twenty: Transition to a New Country and a New Life   103

Chapter Twenty-one: You Can Have the Boys!   109

Chapter Twenty-two: Chamo   114

Chapter Twenty-three: Near Death!   116

Chapter Twenty-four: Pickles or Mustard?   123

Chapter Twenty-five: I Can See!   126

Chapter Twenty-six: Don't Leave Your Keys in the Door!   129

Chapter Twenty-seven: Anecdotes: Thank You, God!   132
My Lucky Day! / More of God's Blessings

Chapter Twenty-eight: Travel Delights and Travel Plights   138

Chapter Twenty-nine: A Teacher's Legacy or Life in God's Service   147

Chapter Thirty: Final Chapter   154

Chapter Thirty-one: God is... Bible Verse Chapter   157

My Three Lives

They say cats have nine lives. Well, I have had three lives. Before I take you on my daughters' and my journeys, I need to explain the organization of this book. I take you on our adventures by offering stories—from silly to serious—of our time in the United States, then in Mexico, and later back in the United States. I have divided the book into three sections that correspond to what I consider my three lives. *My First Life*, or *Part One*, is my growing up in the United States—mainly in Wisconsin. That comprises my first nineteen years. I do not go into as much detail here, as this part of my life is possibly more typical of your own. However, it is necessary to include this, as it will become evident later that the way parents raise their children can have a definite impact on how the children think and behave later. *My Second Life*, or *Part Two*, is my time in Mexico. Here, it gets interesting. I meet my special someone, get married, have my **three** wonderful daughters, all gifts from God. Life here definitely is an adventure for my daughters and me. There are many wonderful times, but life can also be a bumpy road. After twenty-two years of this, it was time to embark on another quest—this time for happiness and fulfillment for my daughters and me back in the United States. This constitutes *My Third Life*, or *Part Three*, which continues to this day.

Besides sharing our life stories with you, I have three more purposes for this book. I want to be a witness of God, of Jesus. This is my opportunity to do so. These are our stories; they are the means by which our faith can shine through. Also, sharing these stories is the perfect way to leave a legacy for my family through their family history, my third purpose. Ultimately, I also hope to inspire you to find a way to leave a legacy for your own family.

My strong faith and love of my family are the common threads throughout this book. They are what I live for—my "raison d'être." My daughters and I often get together and reminisce on many of the things that we have experienced. Then we laugh and say we should write a book about them. Well, this is that book, and I invite you to join us on this journey.

My desire is for these pages to be a testament to the enduring power of faith and the unbreakable bonds of family. This book is a journey through the chapters of our lives, a tapestry woven from the threads of our experiences in two different worlds, the US and Mexico. This is our story of resilience, love, and the unshakeable belief that God is our protector, our refuge, our rock, our fortress, and our anchor in the stormy seas of life. Through our family history, I shine a light on the profound importance of faith. It is the cornerstone our lives are built on, our source of our greatest joys, our solace in challenging times, our motivation, and our purpose for the future.

As you read these stories, take time to appreciate and enjoy the beautiful moments that God has made possible for you, and, if you are experiencing adversity, anxiety, doubt, physical or financial difficulties, understand that we can give it to God and let God help us through our struggles. We need to pray for God's protection, strength, healing, and love, and we can take comfort knowing God is in control. There is a deep peace that faith in God can bring us. We are never alone. God is always with us, our constant companion, guiding us in this incredible journey called life.

With this book I leave a legacy for my family through their family history. I also invite you to embrace the values of faith and family and reflect on the legacy that you would like to leave behind for your loved ones. We are all part of a grander story. Through faith and family, we can leave a legacy that can influence and motivate generations to come.

PART ONE

My First Life

GROWING UP IN
THE UNITED STATES:
NINETEEN YEARS
(1951–1969)

CHAPTER ONE

When? Where? To Whom?

"Thank you, God, for when I was born, where I was born, and to whom!" I say this every day, and I mean it. I'm one of those baby boomers born after World War II—1951, actually. Where? I grew up in Green Bay, Wisconsin, living there from kindergarten until I was nineteen years old—the start of my second life. To whom? The most perfect parents God could have given me. (More on them later.)

I am so thankful for this first part of my life.

I hope through me you can experience a little of what it was like to grow up in Green Bay back then. I praise God every day for blessing me with this time and place, and with my parents, and I see Him in every situation. I hope I can inspire you to look for ways God is expressing His love for you, and ways you experience God in your daily life, too. God does exist, and He is good.

We were a close-knit, middle-class family of the 1950s and '60s. My childhood was quite idyllic. Our family had a strong faith, and we children were taught to be respectful and polite to everyone. Dad was the breadwinner, and Mom stayed home and took care of us children. We played outside most of the time. We were free to ride our bikes wherever we wanted; there was a gigantic cliff across the street to the left of our house and a huge, wide-open space directly in front, beyond which was a fascinating, tree-lined creek. That field gave the children plenty of room to play, and the cliff and creek provided us with amazing places to explore.

"Mom, look what I found!" That was my brother, Tom. He had just found a huge, old skull from some animal while he was digging on that cliff. My mother never knew what he would bring home.

"Mom, look at these arrowheads." He found many obsidian arrowheads that the Native Americans had left there. We liked to try to imagine what it was like back when Native Americans roamed the plains. Many rocks also made their way to our home for Tom's growing rock collection.

The creek was our happy place. There was an apple tree at the top of the path leading down to the creek. I wonder if it had been planted by Johnny Appleseed during the time of his wanderings. It could have been. The apples weren't very sweet, but it was fun climbing the tree to pick them, anyway. Down below, all of us children loved to explore the creek and its surroundings. We walked along the fallen trees that formed bridges we used to cross to the other side of the water, checking out the dams made by beavers. My brother explored miles of that creek, and came home one day excited, but scared. He said he saw a pipe coming out of the riverbank where he had gone, and blood was pouring out of it. We found out later that it was from one of the meatpacking plants.

When we weren't playing outside, we were playing with our friends in our basement, or at their houses, or playing board games with our parents. During more peaceful moments, we were probably watching TV, especially if Mom was cleaning the house or folding clothes. The kids' shows back then were wholesome family shows. We watched *Leave It To Beaver, Lassie, Father Knows Best, I Love Lucy,* and *The Adventures of Ozzie and Harriet.* The lifestyle of those families was very different from many current lifestyles. However, just as Dad was the breadwinner in our family, the dads were in charge in these television shows, and the women took care of the family and the house. And the children were polite and respectful. It was a peaceful time, and I thank God for letting me grow up then. I was blessed.

Besides those family shows, we loved to watch Westerns. There were so many that were fun to watch: *The Rifleman, Bonanza, Gunsmoke, The Lone Ranger, Rawhide . . .* I can still hum the theme songs to some of them. John Wayne was a staple in the movies, as was Ronald Reagan.

"Waaaaa!" That was my brother starting to cry out loud when we were watching the movie *Heidi* with Shirley Temple. I was sitting behind him in the living room when he started crying loudly. I'll never forget it. Tom was two years younger than I was. He was probably about six years old at the time. I don't blame him for crying. I was crying silently, too. The movie was sad.

We loved to watch any movie with Shirley Temple in it. (*The Little Princess, The Little Colonel, Fort Apache . . .*) That little girl sure could sing and dance. And she had the cutest smile, and the blondest, curliest hair.

My mom liked to watch soap operas. *As The World Turns* was her favorite. She watched it while she was cleaning. She mopped the linoleum floors of the dining room, kitchen, and breezeway on her knees. We had better not step on her wet floors, or we'd surely get yelled at, and rightly so. It was hard work to clean the floors like that.

My chores were to clean my room and the bathroom. I would also help with yard work in the summer and shoveling snow in the winter. My brother and I would get a small allowance for our help.

I remember Dad in his office listening to country music, smoking his pipe, and doing his paperwork for his sales for whatever company he was working for at the time. The cherry aroma of his tobacco filled the air. He loved sales—and he was good at it. He won many awards for his successes.

While Dad was working in his office, I oftentimes practiced the piano. It was right there next to him. My parents wanted me to learn to play well, and they paid me a whole ten cents for every half hour I practiced. They took me to piano lessons once a week. My brother said he never wanted to have the piano teacher I had. She was very strict. The very first class I had with her, she cut and filed down my nails. She said there was no way I could play well with long nails. And she had a ruler she wasn't afraid to use to hit my fingers if I was doing something wrong. I did learn to play well, though, and competed in music contests when I was in high school.

Another memory of my dad was of him sitting on a little brown bench shining all our shoes. He loved to do that for us. I think that was relaxing for him, and it made him happy.

At twelve years old, I babysat for the neighbors who lived across the street from us. They always had lots of dirty dishes, and I'd wash them after I put their son to bed. They paid me two dollars an hour, and Mom went over to their house and told them they were paying me too much. Can you imagine? I was not incredibly happy about that.

I loved school. Music was one of my favorite classes. I was first flutist in the band and loved playing during our concerts, and marching and playing at the football games, as well as in parades. I can still remember Mr. Huntsberger, my band director, and one of my favorite teachers in high school, moving his index finger up and down directing us, and really feeling the music. Those were fun times.

My other favorite class was Spanish. I started learning Spanish in seventh grade. Seventh and eighth grade Spanish counted as one year of high school Spanish for us, so I started with tenth grade Spanish when I started high school in ninth grade. I finished all the Spanish classes that were offered in my high school when I was a junior, but when I approached my senior year, I still wanted to continue learning. My parents came to an agreement with my high school wherein I could go to the University of Wisconsin Green Bay campus after school to take a Spanish class, and the high school would pay for all expenses. I did, and I ended up taking a college junior-level literature course. I had six college credits of Spanish when I graduated from high school (and six credits of college English, too).

I graduated from high school in 1969. I was blessed with a scholarship and a Pell grant, so I was ready to go off and face the world. I had been torn between going into music or Spanish, and I decided I wanted to become a Spanish teacher. I had wanted to go to either the University of Texas at Austin or the University of Wisconsin at Madison, both top-ten universities at that time for Spanish.

"Stay in-state and go to a university here, and with the money you would save from out-of-state tuition, you could study in Mexico for a summer session." That was the advice of my Spanish teacher, Mr. Busot, an emigrant who escaped from Cuba and was teaching at the University of Wisconsin in Green Bay. I took his advice and finally chose to go to Whitewater State University in Wisconsin to become that Spanish teacher. In the summer of 1970, I was on my very first plane ride, flying to Mexico City to take classes at the Universidad Iberoamericana, along with other students from Whitewater State in a program organized especially for us to earn college credits and learn about Mexican culture by living with a host family. I stayed in a home at Heriberto Frías Street #827 with five other girls from my home university: Bonnie, Connie, Terri, Kathy, and Pat. That was quite an experience. Our host family was really only taking us in for the money and did not pay much attention to us. Thank God we had each other.

For supper sometimes all we got was a bowl of cold cereal and a glass of milk, or we would have one little chicken divided up among the six of us. I was glad I knew how to ask for which piece of chicken I wanted. "*Quisiera un muslo*," ("I would like a thigh.") I would say. Poor Terri. She would always get a wing. After our paltry dinner, we would have to go downstairs and around the corner to a taco place to get more to eat. And then, in class I'd sit by a guy from our group who would talk about how his host family took him to the zoo or other places, and how they'd have steak dinners and other delicious foods. I didn't feel quite as blessed at those times.

But I was blessed. God was good to me, and I was grateful. I thank Him every day for when I was born, where I was born, and to whom, and for everything that God made possible for me.

I hope we all can see the positive in our circumstances and feel our "God moments," experience God in our daily lives. It's easy when everything is going great. It's a bit more challenging when hardships appear. However, God is with us, even in adversity. That will be part of my life number two . . .

Two Amazing People, Blessings from God

Love the Lord your God with all your heart and with all your soul and with all your strength. These commandments that I give you today are to be in your hearts. Impress them on your children. Talk about them when you sit at home and when you walk along the road, when you lie down and when you get up.

Deuteronomy 6:5-7

How I wish my parents could be here right now. I have so many questions for them. They are the reason I am what I am today. They have always been there for me, always supported me, even when they had their doubts about what I was getting myself into at times. I thank God every day for having bestowed the gift of these remarkable people on me.

Theirs was a real love story. My dad, Robert Waltman, was born on August 16, 1925. My mom, Janice Wickesberg, was born on the fifteenth of June of the same year. Dad always loved to joke that he married an older woman (she was two months older). They stayed married for fifty-eight years, until my dad died in 2006. The family was concerned about my mom's will to live after Dad's passing, as my parents had been so happily married for so long. However, our tight, loving family, Mom's faith, and the knowledge that she'd see Dad again in Heaven kept her going.

Grandma Waltman and Me

Dad grew up in Appleton, Wisconsin, where he was born. His father, Frank Waltman, died when dad was twelve, and his mother, Olga Dahms Waltman, never remarried. Her father helped her with what he could to bring up my dad and his brother Frank, and my grandmother rented out part of the house to also help with the expenses. Dad worked at different jobs as a teenager. I know he worked in a movie theater and for the Heinz company. Any catsup we would use had to be Heinz, and he put it on almost everything.

When Dad was seventeen, World War II was in full swing, and the spirit of patriotism abounded. Dad was so anxious to do his service for his country that he enlisted at that age. He was a ham radio operator during the war. He never wanted to tell us stories about those years until he was older; then he told us a few. One was about a time he was riding in the back of his jeep, next to the radio, when they made a stop. Dad got out of the back to buy some cigarettes, and the jeep took off without him. I don't know how he got back to where they had been stationed ,but thank the Lord they didn't need his services and didn't even realize he had been left behind. Another story he told was of a time they had gone to a village in Germany to get the villagers to surrender. He was very happy that the day before his unit arrived, the residents had been forced to give up their weapons, so Dad's unit had it easy. I really wish my dad were here to tell me more details. He served in the army from 1943 to 1945. He was in the Battle of the Bulge and considered it a real honor to have stood guard at the hospital door of the famous four-star General George S. Patton in the general's final days after his freak car accident on the German autobahn. Dad said he even helped to turn General Patton's body several times so he wouldn't get bedsores.

My mom grew up in the small town of Black Creek, Wisconsin. Her father, Launce Wickesberg, and mother, Viola Grunwaldt, had five children: Mom, Joyce, Bruce, Don, and Jerry, so Mom came from a much bigger family than my dad did. My grandfather was a letter carrier, and my grandmother was a homemaker. Being a letter carrier at that time entailed much more than simply delivering letters. Grandpa used to deliver  live chickens, rabbits, and other interesting things, too. They had a big, beautiful house with many apple trees that we loved to climb when we were growing up, and a gigantic garden full of all kinds of fruits and vegetables. We kids used to go and pick raspberries for them when we'd visit, but we didn't have many to take to them, as we usually ate most of them ourselves.

When it came time for my mom to go to high school, she wanted to go to school in Appleton, Wisconsin, a big city compared to the town of Black Creek, where she grew up. This turned out to be a crucial decision that changed the trajectory of her life. There she met my dad. She always said that they had been in the same homeroom for years, as she was a Wickesberg, and he was a Waltman, and homerooms were organized alphabetically. However, she never really paid any attention to him until he got back from the war. Then, one evening they were at a dance, and Dad asked her to dance, and that started what was to become a wonderful romance and a very happy marriage of almost six decades—until my dad died. They went on to create a loving family with one son and two daughters.

I was the oldest of the children. My brother Tom followed two years later, and my sister Nancy followed five years after that. I was closest to my brother, as we were only two years apart. We covered for each other at times, but my brother was  much wilder than I was. He always said he was glad that I went before him to soften our parents, and I was always glad that I preceded him at school so that the teachers didn't know him before me. When I went away to Whitewater State University, my sister was eleven years old, so I was never as close to her as I was to my brother.

Tom, Nancy, and I were very fortunate to have such wonderful, God-loving parents. I thank the Lord every day for having blessed us with the perfect parents for us. They were there for us every step of the way.

"I'll need some parents to volunteer to bring refreshments/prizes for our field trip/ Christmas show . . ." Up would go my hand. I was always volunteering my mom and dad. The teachers used to tell my mom that they had to look away and try to get other volunteers, too.

And volunteer my mom did. She volunteered at our schools. She volunteered at our church. And she volunteered us, too. We would be part of the various shows the church would put on. I remember being at church holding the American flag and singing patriotic songs on stage with friends of mine for a program my mom helped direct. I also remember singing "I Saw Mommy Kissing Santa Claus" and "All I Want for Christmas Is My Two Front Teeth" (that I happened to be missing) at a school Christmas program, my parents in the front row beaming. I especially  remember having a winter party at our house every year that I was in Brownies and Girl Scouts. My mom was a den mother and would have the Scouts over to the house for hot chili soup and crackers after we had finished ice skating on the frozen creek across the field from our house. Those days were always special.

Back to my dad. He graduated from St. Louis University's Parks Air College and would take my mom up in the sky. He piloted many small planes, but he soon stopped because his ears couldn't take the air pressure changes. He then became a salesperson of a variety of things. He sold chemical and industrial supplies, life insurance, and even Kaypro computers. He loved being a salesperson. He loved being outside and having the liberty to plan his own hours.

Before her marriage, my mom worked as a secretary at Kimberly

Clark and was always fond of saying that. Whenever we'd go to a bathroom or any place else where there were Kimberly Clark hand towel dispensers, etc., she'd tell us that she had worked for that company. After getting married, Mom was a homemaker until I went away to the university. Then she started working at the University of Wisconsin in Green Bay, where they were living at the time. She worked there for two years before they moved to El Paso, Texas, where she worked at the University of Texas at El Paso from 1972 until she retired in 1989. She started working as a secretary in the Biology department. Then, she switched over to Language Arts as a senior secretary. She was the personal secretary of Dr. Diana Natalicio when Dr. Natalicio became the head of the Department of Language Arts. She later became the president of the whole University of Texas at El Paso. As president, Dr. Natalicio invited Mom and Dad to her house every year when she gave a party for UTEP professors. When Mom retired, she was given a special party and an award for her service. Then she was blessed with thirty years of retirement to enjoy her family and friends.

My parents loved Green Bay, but they had wanted to move because of the intense winters. After I got married and went to live in Mexico City in 1970, they made that big move to El Paso, Texas, which was great because then they were much closer to me.

The Green Bay Packers was their team. Mom and Dad had season tickets to the games, and they loved every game—even the ones played in below-zero weather and it was snowing. They really had to bundle up in multiple layers of wool clothing to stay warm. But you know, "Once a Packer backer, always a Packer backer," whether they won or lost, and even when my parents lived in Texas, the home of the Dallas Cowboys, they stayed true to their team. Actually, we are all still Packer backers.

My parents were devoted Christians and superb examples for us to follow. We all went to church every Sunday and attended all its festivities. I sang in the choir. My mom helped whenever and wherever she could. At home, we ate breakfasts and dinners together every day at the dining room table, but we had to keep our conversations very tame. Dad didn't even like us to talk about frogs. We did as many things as we could together as a family. We lived in the Midwest Bible Belt and lived our lives accordingly. What was that like? Read along.

The family's greatest tradition was making Christmas sugar cookies together. My mom would bake dozens of them beforehand, and then we'd all sit down at the dining room table and use our artistic abilities to create interestingly decorated cookies using a variety of sugar colors and candy shapes. We seemed like a family right out of a Norman Rockwell painting. My sister's family and my family still carry on this tradition.

As a family, we loved to play board games together. However, bridge was the preferred game of my parents with their friends. They had a couple of groups of friends they would get together with at each other's houses. My brother, sister, and I loved it when they played at our house. Mom always served the chocolate bridge mix candies and other snacks, and she would put the leftovers in little baggies and place them under our pillows. What an incentive to behave while they were playing cards.

My brother, sister, and I would usually play games or do other things in the basement, which was the same size as the house. Tom, Nancy, and I each had a corner. Tom had his gigantic rock collection in his. Nancy and I had girl toys in our section. We had a ping-pong table at one end and a gigantic wooden table in the middle (where the Girl Scouts and I would have the previously mentioned parties with the chili soup after ice skating, and where all of Mom's family and we would eat for Thanksgiving and Christmas get-togethers).

Almost every summer the whole family would spend a week up north at the Christian camp called Camp Luther in Three Lakes, Wisconsin. My grandpa and Kathryn (his wife after my grandma died) would go along with us. We kids loved this place. We would stay in a cottage right on the lake. We'd take a small boat and row all around the connected lakes. Everything was so beautiful. Mom would take us out fishing. (Dad didn't really like to fish.) Sometimes they'd bring my cousin Jerilyn along, too. She and I loved cleaning the fish and cutting open their stomachs to see what they had eaten. And we'd all (except my grandparents) go swimming by the pier. We loved that, too, except that we had to check our bodies carefully for bloodsuckers after each time. Then we'd sprinkle salt on them and watch them shrivel up. When Tom and I grew older, Mom and Dad would send us up to Camp Luther a week before they would go, so we could participate in the youth program where we'd have archery, arts and crafts, bonfires with s'mores, campfire songs, and so much more. A fun memory: the camp had a "Mirror Lake" that they told us had no bottom. There were bogs alongside it with wooden paths we could walk on; we'd look for carnivorous Venus flytrap plants and try to see what they had "eaten." Imagine that! Many years later, Tom often commented that he'd like to go back there someday.

We also took many trips together all over the US. Dad always said we needed to know our own country before we went elsewhere, and we all loved to travel. We did go outside the country to Canada, however, during our trip to Washington state with Dad in 1966, as he had a Kiwanis convention he was sent to when he was serving as Lieutenant Governor of the Wisconsin-Upper Michigan District of Kiwanis International. I liked that he was involved in Kiwanis. I think it was too bad that the actual club meetings then were only for the men, but they had so many fun parties and picnics for the whole family, too.

As you can see, we were a very close-knit family. Even after I went away to college, and then got married and moved to Mexico, and Tom went away to college, met his future wife, Nasrin, in Houston, and eventually moved out to California to form his own family with her, his daughter, Roya, and his son, Robert, we all remained as close as possible. My sister Nancy continued living in El Paso with my parents until she met her now-husband, Frank. They had their daughter, Jennifer, and their son, Ryan, and still live in El Paso. I know we have all been blessed in so many ways, and I thank God every day for this.

The profound significance of faith and family that my parents instilled in us, as well as the lifestyle that they worked so hard for us to have, all influenced my brother, my sister, and me as to how we were to conduct ourselves in the future. As I concluded in the prologue, through faith, family, and memories, we can leave a legacy that can influence and motivate generations to come. That is what happened to us, as you shall see in the following stories. My parents left us a great legacy, and now it is up to us to reflect on the legacy that we want to leave behind for our loved ones.

And this is the close of my "first life," my younger years lived in Wisconsin—the first nineteen years of my life. Soon a door would be opened to a totally different life, a life full of happiness, but also with its difficult, challenging, trying moments. Even throughout those moments, I know God was with me. He is with us, and that is a comforting, encouraging reality. We can find happiness and solace with Him. And God is our doorkeeper. And with God, my second life began . . .

PART TWO

My Second Life

LIFE IN MEXICO
(MEXICO CITY, OAXACA,
TUXTLA GUTIERREZ,
AND TAPACHULA):
TWENTY–TWO YEARS
(1970–1992)

CHAPTER THREE

A New Door Opened

And we know that all things work together for good to them that love God, to them who are the called according to His purpose.

Romans 8:28

My first door had not closed, but more doors opened. I had many choices to make, and, as the character in Robert Frost's poem "The Road Not Taken" did, so did I choose the path less trodden on. And that definitely did make all the difference.

As I mentioned in my first life, I had made the choice to choose an in-state university in order to use the money I would save from out-of-state tuition to participate in a summer-in-Mexico program. That was a critical decision that resulted in a complete change in my life.

"OK, girls, we need to decide if we want to go to Acapulco, Guerrero, or Oaxtepec, Morelos, for our Fourth of July four-day break," began the discussion of the six of us girls that were staying together with our host family in Mexico City.

"Well, if we go to Oaxtepec now, we can go to Acapulco after we finish our studies and stay there longer."

That made sense. Acapulco was much more famous. We'd rather spend more time there. We really didn't know what to expect in Oaxtepec, Morelos. Those were our choices for our summer program. Our university would arrange to take us to either place. Some students chose

Acapulco. We chose Oaxtepec, that road less traveled. And the rest is history. That is where I met the man who was to become my husband, and we were married one month later (yes, ONE MONTH LATER) in a civil ceremony in Mexico. A month later, we were saying our vows in my church in Wisconsin. (More on that later.)

That bus to Oaxtepec was full of excited students wondering what adventures would await us at our destination. Tourism is the main business in Oaxtepec, and we were ready to explore what was available and to have some fun. In the evening, after we settled in and were ready to relax, it was off to the hotel's bar to check out what was going on. Where else could we go at that time of the day? All six of us stayed together and formed a big circle to sit and chat. Not long after, the server brought us some drinks and said they were from the guys in the corner. Well, of course, we were curious about those "guys in the corner." We were looking over at them. They were looking over at us. One guy in particular caught my eye. He had the biggest smile and the most beautiful eyes—and he was wearing white socks. That shows how immature I was, I guess. I was infatuated with those white socks. (No guy in the States would be wearing white socks at that time. Dark socks were in.)

Well, it wasn't long before those guys came over and asked if they could join us. And then they did. The guy I had had my eye on sat across from me, but soon he moved and sat right next to me. He was definitely charismatic and interesting. He and his partner were there building the main Oaxtepec bus terminal. They were architects who lived in Mexico City and commuted to Oaxtepec, about sixty miles away, to supervise the construction. They would be going back to Mexico City after the weekend.

"Would you like to go to the *mercado* (market) here tomorrow morning with me for breakfast? I can pick you up. Just say when," he asked me.

Well, we were there to explore and learn about the culture. I agreed and was ready the next morning for another adventure. And adventure it was. I had never gone to a Mexican mercado. How exciting to see all the colorful stands full of fresh fruits and vegetables—some I had never seen before. And then there was the row of *carniceros* (butchers) preparing every cut of meat a person could desire, their knives clicking on their cutting boards. We walked over to where the cooked foods were, and my friend Fernando ordered some cooked pork and some cooked beef, a kilo of tortillas, and salsas. We walked over to some wooden tables and benches and ate to our hearts' content. As we were walking back to his car, he gave all the leftovers he had wrapped up— and there were a lot of them—to a lone little boy and told him to enjoy them. That impressed me. And then, a little further on, Fernando saw a person who was wearing those rubber *huaraches* (sandals) made out of tires, and he asked the person if he'd trade those huaraches for his leather boots. Of course, that man was super ecstatic about the trade. And there went Fernando, happy with his cheap sandals. I couldn't believe it! What kind of man was he? I was intrigued.

Before I headed back to Mexico City with our group, Fernando and I exchanged phone numbers. A few days later, when we were all in the D.F. (Mexico City, the Distrito Federal) I got the call. He wondered if I'd go on a date with him. I agreed, but I said I wouldn't go alone with him. My good friend Bonnie and I double dated with Fernando and his partner Martin. Our first date was front-row seats at a boxing match. That was something I certainly had never imagined myself doing.

Bonnie and I continued double dating with that formidable duo whenever we could without letting our studies suffer. Needless to say, we had a lot of fun together. It no longer mattered that our host family didn't feed us or take us places. Fernando and Martin enjoyed showing us around Mexico City. They also took us to Queretaro, Guanajuato,

San Miguel de Allende, and Dolores Hidalgo. They were proud of their country and loved being our tour guides.

During that time, I went with Fernando to meet his family several times. They all seemed to like me. And his *Tía Ceci* (Aunt Ceci) turned out to be quite an *alcahueta* (match maker). She kept telling Fernando, "You shouldn't let Susan get away. She's a keeper!" How embarrassing. But then he took her advice to heart and proposed to me. I was shocked. I didn't know what to say. And then, when Martin heard about what his friend had done, he proposed to Bonnie. I guess she was the only level-headed person of the four of us. She said no. And I said yes! Can you believe it? I was only nineteen years old. Fernando and I really liked each other, and he was right. If we were to make plans and I were to go back to the States, that would probably be the last time we would see each other. And he really wanted to make it official. He arranged a big celebration in his hometown of Lerma, Estado de Mexico, for a civil ceremony. Many of his relatives and friends had to make the long drive from Mexico City to attend. Many more from Lerma also attended. Bonnie had already returned to Wisconsin, so I was the only one on my side. This civil ceremony took place almost exactly one month after we had met. Talk about being impetuous. However, things did work out, and we remained married for twenty-two years, most of them happy.

Can you imagine what my parents must have thought? They sure never expected anything like that to happen with my trip abroad. I never told them about my civil ceremony wedding. I know they would have felt bad that I had done something like that without them. And I didn't really feel married. I wanted a wedding in my church.

Well, after our civil ceremony, Fernando and I took the train from Mexico City up to El Paso, as my parents had been on a trip with my sister and brother and were going to meet us there. As soon as we got there, my parents wanted to meet him. This took place at the hotel where they were staying. There, Fernando told my parents, "I want to marry with HIM!" My sister's eyes opened as wide as donuts. She was twelve at the time, and to hear that certainly surprised her.

After they met Fernando, he went back to Mexico City, and I continued with my family back to Green Bay. One month later, I was getting married in my church, Our Savior Lutheran Church, by Pastor Glock, the same pastor who had given me my first communion. But before that, I had a bridal shower given to me by my friend Ann Sorenson, and another one from my friend Chris Bader. My relatives also organized one for me at my Aunt Joyce's house, and I had a bridal luncheon. People really made arrangements quickly.

"You look amazing," my mother told me. "I got married in that wedding dress, and then your Aunt Joyce did, too. And now, you." I felt so blessed. What a marvelous memory—to have worn my mother's wedding dress. (My sister Nancy even wore it for her wedding, later.) And my veil, with its *migajón* (hand-made bread dough) flower decorations, and my bouquet and lasso,

made of the same material, were made by a cousin of Fernando's. Fernando's Tía Aurora was the *madrina del lasso,* or Godmother of the Lasso. (Which was a tradition I was not familiar with, being a Lutheran. The wedding lasso, or rope, is placed around the shoulders of the couple during the ceremony to join them together in the eyes of God.)

We had a big wedding. Fernando's parents and his Tía Aurora flew in. Fernando's friend Martin, his brother Agustin, and he drove all the way from Mexico City to Green Bay in a little Renault. Everybody arrived safely, and soon we were getting married. Remember Bonnie, my friend who had dated Martin? Well, she was my maid of honor, and Martin was our best man. Fernando's brother Agustin and my brother Tom were groomsmen, and my cousin Jerilyn and my sister were my bridesmaids.

It was such a beautiful wedding. I couldn't have asked for more. But there was more. Mom and Dad had organized a fantastic wedding reception at a venue right on Lake Michigan. All my relatives and so many friends attended. The food was scrumptious, and the music was terrific. And the view of the sunset over the water was fabulous.

And who takes her honeymoon with her husband, her brother-in-law, and her best man? Well, I did. After the wedding, we decided to travel in Martin's car. Fernando and I used the money people had given us as presents and combined it with the money he had to cover our expenses, and off we all went. Meanwhile, my poor mother was left boxing up all my stuff. I owe her so much. As I said at the beginning of my story, my parents were always there for me, always supportive, even when they really wondered about me. I was so blessed. Thank you, God! When Mom had finished packing, and it was time, she mailed all those boxes to Eagle Pass, Texas, where we were going to pick them up when we got there. Would you believe she packed up nine gigantic boxes of my things?

And while my mom was boxing up my things, I was having the time of my life traveling around the country in that little Renault with three men. We visited Oshkosh, Wisconsin; Chicago, Illinois; Niagara Falls, Ontario; and Toronto, Canada. We also traveled to New York City; visited relatives of Martin in Jersey City, New Jersey; then visited Washington, D. C. and New Orleans before arriving at Eagle Pass to pick up all the boxes Mom had sent there.

There were nine big boxes, and we were four adults in a little Renault. We devised the perfect plan. We got the boxes through customs and into Piedras Negras, Mexico, the sister city of Eagle Pass. Then we got two bus tickets and checked in all those boxes. Either Fernando and I or Martin and Agustin drove the Renault, and the two not in the car traveled in the bus. At bus stops, we would change positions. We did this all the way to Mexico City, where we were able to pick up all those boxes. Ingenious, right?

And after this another door was to open...

As I mentioned earlier, my intent telling my story is to illustrate that God is with us, and we can depend on Him. He gave us free will, and I definitely used mine, but He is also our protector, and I certainly gave Him opportunities to protect me. I have no doubt that God is with me always. God is good.

CHAPTER FOUR

A Piano Before a Stove

Picture this: Two newlyweds in the husband's parents' home sitting in the living room with nine big boxes of items belonging to the new daughter-in-law. The boxes are opened, and there are articles of clothing and other personal items strewn everywhere in that small room. The newlyweds have nowhere to stay, so they are hoping to stay with El Doctor Saúl and Aurorita, the husband's parents. What must those parents be thinking right then? And what are the newlyweds thinking?

Well, there Fernando and I were in my in-laws' residence in the Colonia Escandón subdivision in Mexico City. Their "house" was on the first floor, which is what the floor above the ground floor is called in most countries. Below them were businesses and a small market. There was a big *zaguan*, or entrance, to go upstairs to their living quarters. They had a cozy home. And then there were the stairs to the roof. The view from the rooftop was fascinating, as we could watch the vehicles below coming and going, and the hustle and bustle of people conducting their daily business and doing their errands. Everything was so new to me: the type of buildings, my in-laws, the conducting of daily activities in Spanish. How exciting! This door to a new life had opened. And I was anxious to get started.

My mother-in-law was a fabulous cook. Everyone raved about her food. I had never learned to make anything more than a few easy desserts. I didn't even know that milk rises when it is boiled (and can make a real mess boiling over). Now, I wanted to learn to cook like she did. Mexican food was figuratively and literally foreign to me. During the time I grew up in Wisconsin, there weren't Mexican restaurants. And there weren't Mexicans. About the only Mexicans that were there were the migrants who arrived at harvest time every year to help harvest the farmers' crops, and then they'd leave to look for work elsewhere.

"Aurorita, please teach me how to cook some delicious dishes that you make."

"Sue, I can't tell you how. I cook everything *al tanteo*, meaning that I don't measure anything. I just guess how much of each ingredient to include. If you want to learn, you'll just have to watch me," replied my mother-in-law.

And watch, I did. I got a bench and would sit next to her and watch her every move and write everything down in a little notebook I had for her recipes. It was hard to write good recipes, as I never knew exactly how much of any ingredient she added. I would have to learn to cook al tanteo, or hit or miss, too. Her cooking was all hits. Mine would probably be misses for a while. But to learn how to cook scrumptious Mexican food, there's nothing better than to learn from an expert. I learned how to make enchiladas, chilaquiles, pozole, mole, pierna de cerdo (baked pork leg), tortas, chiles rellenos, tortas Españolas (really not a torta at all, but rather a gigantic omelet made with eggs, potatoes and chopped onions and often eaten cold— it even served as an option as a tapa in bars and restaurants in Spain), so many other ways to cook eggs, and so much more. I did finally learn to be an acceptable cook, but nothing like Aurorita. This ability to watch her cook and get her input was a great advantage of staying with my in-laws for a while. I thank God for giving me this opportunity.

"Sue, get your dirty clothes and those of Fernando. I'm going to show you how to wash them," said my mother-in-law. Was I in for a surprise. Up those stairs to the roof we went. There on one side was a big cement block with a scrub board of the same material built in. I hadn't paid any attention to it before, but now I was looking at it curiously. Aurorita took an item of her clothing and a bar of Zote soap, stood in front of the scrub board, and started wetting the garment, soaping it up, moving it back and forth on the scrub board, and then rinsing and squeezing the water out over and over until there was no soap left in the clothes. Wow! That looked like a lot of work. And I was soon to find out that it was. After I watched her wash several of her things, she had me try. Well, of course, I could. However, it was another question of whether I wanted to, but I didn't have much choice. That was what was going to be expected of me. I did learn, although grudgingly. Washing the sheets was the worst. Imagine trying to get them wet, soap them up, wash them on the scrub board, and rinse them well without having them fall out of the scrub board area and get dirty on the cement floor. That was quite a challenging feat. And then, everything that got washed also had to be hung up on the clotheslines. I sure never imagined myself doing anything like that, since back in Wisconsin I grew up with a clothes washer and dryer. Oh, my God, what had I gotten myself into?

My time with my in-laws was indeed special, as they were very welcoming. I think they were glad my husband thought he was finally ready to settle down, as he had been quite a handful. They weren't so sure about him marrying an American girl, but they were gracious about it. I learned a lot about Mexican people and their culture. My Spanish improved immensely, as I had to speak that language if I wanted to carry on a conversation. And, of course, I got to know my in-laws well, and vice versa.

"Canasta, anyone?" That was the question many weeknights. The four of us would sit down at the dining room table and play canasta together, a perfect way for me to learn the Spanish vocabulary for card games. And it was an enjoyable way to get to know each other. I'm not so sure everyone played by the rules, though...

Fernando's grandmother, Macatita, was an angel. I loved talking with her and listening to her stories. When she was just fifteen years old, she was forced to marry Guadalupe, a much older man. That was during the time of the Mexican Revolution, and young women were married to older, strong men who would be able to protect them from the *revolucionarios* if these fighters invaded the area. Macatita told me of a time she was put in a big barrel to hide her from intruders. It must have been a very scary time.

Later ..."OK, woman, it's time for you to retire. The baptism is over, and the party is about to begin." That was Guadalupe, Macatita's husband, sending her to her room in their house in Lerma, Estado de Mexico, so he and his friends could party. And that was the evening of the baptism of my mother-in-law, Aurora. Needless to say, Macatita was quite bitter about that. Talk about women's rights—women then had none.

Macatita was the person who taught me how to get around in Mexico City. She was a widow by the time we got married, and she had the time and energy to run around with me while Fernando was working. She showed me how to get around by bus, by streetcar, by metro (subway), and by taxi. We walked all around the metropolitan area, and she showed me her favorite stores, how she special-ordered her facial and body creams with the ingredients she wanted in them, as well as historical and other important areas of the city. We would get a bite to eat somewhere downtown, and then off we'd go, back to my in-laws' house. I considered Macatita one of God's angels sent to help me along my way in my new life in Mexico.

An interesting aside: years before, as Macatita's husband Guadalupe was dying in their house in Lerma, he started to tell the people around him that the treasure that they all knew existed and had been hidden during the time of the revolution was under the . . . He never finished his sentence. He died right then. Well, he had people digging all over the place, inside and outside of his house. Nobody ever found it—or at least nobody admitted to finding it. Possibly the people who bought the house and land much later found it. Wouldn't that be something? There are probably still people's treasures buried in different places throughout Mexico.

Fernando mostly behaved well while we lived that month or two with my in-laws. He had to be careful not to anger his father. While we were still staying with El Doctor and Aurorita, Fernando arrived at their house one day and announced, "*Mujer, adivina lo que te compré.*" ("Woman, guess what I bought you.") And, to my surprise, it was a beautiful piano. He knew I played the piano and was excited to give me something special, so yes, I did have a piano before a stove.

Now, how were we going to get that piano up into his parents' house and store it until we found a place to live? What a conundrum. But we did. And soon we found just the perfect spot for us to settle down; it was even more of a challenge to get that piano down the steep, stone path to that remarkable place...

CHAPTER FIVE

Our Perfect Place

"Yikes. It's a scorpion. I thought it was just a glob of dirt."

I screamed that after I realized what I had been looking at. I had gotten up that night to take care of personal business, and while I was preparing to wash my hands, I was peering closely at something I saw in the sink. I hadn't put my glasses on, so I really couldn't see it clearly. I almost had my face right by its tail before I realized what it was. And yes, there were scorpions in our perfect place. Little black ones.

Even so, the place we found in the *Desierto de los Leones* was the perfect place for us. It was high on a hill on the outskirts of Mexico City. On a clear day, at the top of the hill we had an amazing view of a large part of the DF. (Distrito Federal, or Federal District). You may wonder why that area is called the Desierto de los Leones. It is not a desert or deserted. It is a forest full of pine trees. And *los Leones* does not refer to lions. León was the last name of the family back in the colonial times that was able to get permission from Spain for the monks to use that area for the construction of their monastery. This area is now best known for that monastery and the lush park areas with great hiking trails and picnic areas.

Our apartment was located on the street Olivar de los Padres. The apartments in our complex were constructed down the side of a hill. A winding, stone path took us from the parking area at the top to half-way down the hill, passing all the entrances along the way. Our apartment was the last one down the path. The entrance to a racket ball court was just about fifteen steps to the side of where we lived, the walls of the court hidden by a multitude of tall trees. Just below our place was a steep *barranca*, or cliff. And yes, it was quite a trek to go up and down that stone path to get to and from our house. And it was a definite challenge to get that beautiful piano my husband bought me into our house, but they managed.

All around the grounds of our complex were trees, trees, and more trees. Birds were constantly singing their cheerful songs. Colorful flowers bloomed all over. It was an idyllic place. We were in the middle of a forest. God's hand was evident everywhere. It seemed like we were in heaven.

This was our first home, and we loved it. The grounds were amazing. The fresh air was especially wonderful, a great contrast to the polluted air within Mexico City itself. We lived in a one-bedroom, one all-purpose room, and one-bathroom apartment, which was fine by us. We didn't have many things, anyway. Fernando built our bed and put up some simple shelves. And yes, we had our piano.

Surprise. My neighbor right above me was American. She was from California, but I didn't even know she was American for several months. I can't even remember how we started talking to each other and realized we were compatriots, but we became close friends. Liz was her name, and Willy was her husband. We all got along very well and did a variety of things together. It was fantastic to have someone to speak English with. I really hadn't spoken English since I moved to Mexico except to talk to my family by phone. It's funny how easy it is to forget simple words and phrases when you don't use your language. I couldn't remember how to say, "*Sube la ventana.*" ("Roll up the car window.") I couldn't remember how to say *toronja* (grapefruit). It all came back, though, once I started conversing with Liz. I'm still friends with her. She now lives in California. I thank God for our friendship.

Terrific. My family was going to visit me. I was so excited. I was six months pregnant and anxiously awaiting the arrival of our little one. Fernando and I enjoyed taking my family around to show them this beautiful country. We had a red Willys jeep, and somehow, we all fit inside. We took them to the Plaza Garibaldi for an exquisite dinner and mariachi music. We took them to the famous Mercado San Juan, where you can buy almost anything. Dad saw a tall, almost five-foot-high carved, wooden statue of Don Quixote. He fell in love with it and decided that he wanted it—and he wanted to show off his newly acquired

vocabulary to ask for it. (He had studied a little Spanish before the trip.)

"*Cuánto cuesta, por favor?*" ("How much does that cost, please?") Wow. We were all impressed, but he wasn't done yet.

"*Quince dólares,*" ("Fifteen dollars.") the merchant replied.

"*Es demasiado caro, HOMBRE, por favor,*" Dad blurted out slowly and proudly with definite emphasis on the word hombre. (Translation: "That's too expensive, man, please.") Well, he ended up taking it with him all the way to Wisconsin, and I am happy to say that now I am the proud keeper of the statue, along with all its memories.

Fernando and I also took my family to the city of Puebla in the state of Puebla, where they say there is a church for every day of the year, although there are really only 288 churches. We took them to Cuernavaca, Morelos, the City of Eternal Spring. There we attended a party of some friends of Fernando's.

"Dad, how do you like those tacos?"

"They're pretty good."

"I just want to let you know that you just ate *tacos de sesos*. Those are tacos of cow brains, a real delicacy."

Poor Dad. He almost choked. He did not appreciate us offering those to him. And soon after, he got Montezuma's Revenge (diarrhea named after the last Aztec ruler as his revenge for being conquered). I don't know if the diarrhea was from the tacos, but it still was very disconcerting for him. Dad gets embarrassed very easily, and he did not enjoy that "revenge." After that, Dad never wanted to go back to Mexico to visit.

It was so very hard to say goodbye to my family, but the time had come. It would be back to two-dollar-a-minute phone calls to keep in touch. Those always got expensive very quickly.

Two months later:

"Help. *Ayúdenme!*" ("Help me!")

That was me early one morning shouting from our racquetball court. About one month after my parents left, when I was seven months pregnant, I had fallen while playing racquetball with myself and sprained my ankle badly. I could hardly get up. And no one came to help. Everyone was gone to work or in their apartments and didn't hear me. After a while, I was able to hobble back to our place (as I mentioned earlier, only about fifteen steps from the court) and put my foot up. I thank the Lord that I didn't get hurt worse and that my baby was ok. I know God was protecting us. That was formally the end of my racquetball playing while pregnant.

But it wouldn't be long until . . .

CHAPTER SIX

Surprise!
Here's Our New Baby!

It was the middle of September of 1971. We were still living in the Desierto de los Leones, that lush, forested area on the outskirts of Mexico City. My husband and I had gone into the city for a visit with my doctor, as I was very pregnant. According to my calculations, made from something I had read, I should be ready to give birth. We thought it prudent to ask my doctor if he thought we could take a trip. You see, there was going to be a big, exciting party in Lerma, Estado de Mexico, and my husband didn't want to miss it. My doctor checked me out and said that we could go, but to go slowly and carefully. We said, "So be it."

The driving distance from Mexico City to Lerma is about thirty-five miles straight. However, what makes it take so long to get there are all the sharp, dangerous curves as one goes up the mountains. We went slowly and carefully and arrived without incident. And then it was time to party. So many of my husband's relatives were there, and the party was at his grandmother's house. I must say, all the guests enjoyed themselves, including me. Mexican food is so delicious—especially prepared in those small towns by real Mexican cooks. I indulged.

"It's pretty late. We better not go back to Mexico City tonight," my husband told me. I agreed.

"Well, we're going to have to stay in the next room, together with my mom and dad and my grandma."

"Wow, that should be interesting," I thought.

"But I didn't bring any clothes to change into," was my reply.

"That's OK, Sue," my mother-in-law said. "We'll find something for you."

They sure did. What they found was a nightgown that belonged to my husband Fernando's grandmother. And she was a hefty woman, so I guess I was quite a sight.

"Ok, we're going to sleep in that bed over there. Mom and Dad will be sleeping in that bed (he pointed to one in a corner). And that's my Grandma Macatita's bed. There will be *biombos*, or folding screens, separating all of us." I opened my eyes wide. I was a bit incredulous, but, again, so be it.

Well, quite a night ensued. My father-in-law, El Doctor, was snoring. My body was aching, and I was rocking back and forth in "our" bed. After a while my husband asked me what the matter was.

"*Me duele mi espalda*," ("My back aches.") I replied. This continued the rest of the night. I couldn't help it. I was very uncomfortable.

In the morning, I took a trip to the bathroom. (This was a typical Mexican house of that time, with a big portion of the house running alongside the sidewalk next to the street. The bathroom was on the side of the porch facing the inside yard but outside the rooms of the house.)

"Uh oh, Honey. I spotted blood."

Well, Aurorita heard that. "*¡Hijo, tu mujer va a tener a su bebé!*" ("I was going to have my baby!") My father-in-law, El Doctor, probably would have realized that sooner had I said at night, "*Me duele la cintura*," ("My waist hurts.") instead of saying that my back hurt.

Anyway, with that, everything was put in motion. There I was wearing my husband's grandmother's nightgown. They slipped my sandals on my feet, and off we went to Lerma's brand-new clinic. They didn't even give me time to put my contacts in so I could see. Due to its being such a new clinic, there was only one doctor. While my husband was calling a hospital in Toluca, the capital of the state of Mexico and only about twenty miles away, trying to find a place to take me there to have my baby, the doctor at the clinic said, "*Esta mujer se queda aquí.*" "She's having her baby." She's staying here. And that was that. I was to stay there. Our precious Jeanette was born. And shortly after that, we were back in Mexico City entering my doctor's office with her in my arms. "SURPRISE, Doctor. Here's our baby!"

As I mentioned in the introduction, my purpose is to illustrate through chosen events in my life how it is evident that God **does** exist. I am convinced that God was with me every step of the way at this time. We arrived at Lerma with no mishaps, even though the road was dangerous and curvy, and I was very pregnant. We decided to stay the night there, even though the accommodations were a bit strange for me. That was a good thing. Had I had the baby on the road, she probably would have died, as her umbilical cord was wrapped around her neck. In Lerma, a capable doctor tended to her, and there were no problems with the birth. Had we driven back to where we lived in the Desierto de los Leones on the outskirts of Mexico City and Jeanette decided to come while I was there, with my husband far away at work, who knows how that would have ended up. God is good.

CHAPTER SEVEN

We Didn't See These Things Coming!

Our perfect place in the Desierto de Los Leones remained just that for about a year and a half. However, with that steep cliff right outside our door, living there became quite dangerous for our daughter Jeanette when she started walking. It was time to move. That way Fernando could also be closer to his work. We found another almost perfect place to live. This time it was in the Colonia Jardines del Pedregal near San Angel, inside Mexico City proper. It was a small, two-bedroom home with a very clever floor plan where the bedrooms and a small living area connecting them could be separated from the rest of the house by closing a door to a short hallway. There was a delightful interior garden that could be admired from the front living room and from the bedrooms and living area in the back, as those areas wrapped around the garden, giving the whole house a sense of peace and happiness. God is good.

I only drove in Mexico City once in the whole three and a half years we lived in the Desierto de los Leones and El Pedregal, as Mexican drivers were to be feared. They drove *"a lo macho,"* which, in this case, meant very aggressively. In Green Bay, while I was there, the population was only about 30,000 people, and the little bit I drove was mostly just near where I lived. Here, in the heart of Mexico City, there were about ten MILLION people at that time. That was a lot to take in for a small-town girl. I was scared just being a passenger. The roundabouts all around the city were HUGE with brave drivers switching lanes everywhere. That was not for me. I was so thankful that Fernando's grandmother had taught me how to get around by bus and metro. And I used that knowledge to take my daughter places while her daddy worked. Mostly we would take the bus to the San Angel parks for our outings. That was fun for both of us. I continuously thanked God for all those wonderful opportunities to do so much with my daughter while we lived there.

One evening at that house:

"Agustín, come here right now. One of your worms is walking across the kitchen floor!" I shouted to my brother-in-law. We were enjoying a peaceful meal at our house in the Pedregal. Agustín was visiting us. Somewhere, he and Fernando had found some *gusanos de maguey* (maguey plant worms), I assume at a market nearby, and proceeded to cook them live—and by that, I mean the worms were alive. I was cooking rice and potatoes. Agustín wanted to show his cooking prowess by preparing the maguey worms. The food was served. We were eating. We had run out of tortillas, so I went to the kitchen to heat some up, when, to my surprise, I saw a little worm scurrying across the kitchen floor trying to save itself from its demise. I'm sure it had already experienced great pain as it hit the frying pan, but it must have flown in the air after hitting the hot oil. Poor thing probably thought it had escaped certain death, but, alas, it had been discovered, and Agustín dealt with it as expected. We sure had a hearty laugh over that incident.

Three things stand out the most about our time there in El Pedregal. The first incident involved our daughter.

"We really need to call a doctor. She's getting sicker and sicker. She has a very high fever. I'm afraid she could die!"

"Dear God, Heavenly Father, please send your angels to surround our little Jeanette with their love and care and put your protection over her," I prayed.

Jeanette was a little over two years old at that time. Her body was limp. Her fever was high. It was so scary. Fernando did go to find a doctor and brought one to the house to see her. The doctor checked her out, gave her a suppository, and we waited. Would you believe Jeanette pooped out a long red balloon? All her suffering was because she had swallowed a balloon. Well, we were certainly relieved that that was all it was. It was an easy solution if you knew what the problem and the solution were. Thank the Lord for great doctors. (An important takeaway from this incident is to pay attention when told not to send balloons into the air. Many birds and other animals are eating pieces of these and suffering the consequences. They are not as fortunate as our daughter was to have a doctor come to their aid.)

The second thing that stands out about our stay in this house in Mexico City involved Fernando's health. He definitely was a macho man (assertive, aggressive, proud of his masculinity). He was also very stubborn. This did not work in his favor with respect to his health.

"Father God, please put your healing hands upon my husband Fernando and help him recover from his pain." More prayers.

"This pain is unbearable. I guess I'll finally have to give up, follow your advice, and go see a doctor. Nothing I have tried has worked. I just can't stand this pain anymore."

That was Fernando, finally giving in to the severe pains he was feeling from his kidney stones. He had tried drinking loads of fluids. He had tried drinking teas people had recommended. He had tried to have those pesky stones zapped. Nothing had worked, so it became time to go under the knife. His father, a doctor, was given permission to observe the procedure. The arrangements were made, and Fernando was ready. The day came, and the doctors talked to my mother-in-law, Aurorita, and me, and then left to take care of my husband. Aurorita and I waited. Finally, the doctors and my father-in-law came out to fill us in on the results. Wow. What a surprise. They had cut open the first two layers of Fernando's skin from the middle of his chest down to almost his belly button. And then they had to sew him back up without finishing. He was bleeding too much. "*Ay, qué sangrón!*" That comment could be taken two ways, and they both applied to Fernando. Literally, "*Qué sangrón*" means that he was a real bleeder. In Spanish, figuratively, "*Qué sangrón!*" means annoying, mean, rude. Well, maybe that didn't really apply to him, but, after all was said and done, this became a real joke about him, even though it wasn't very funny at the moment. We waited for him to come out of recovery. It was as if he had gone through the complete operation. He was really going to be hurting. How were we going to tell him that he was going to have to go through that whole thing again? Can you imagine? I'd be incredulous and quite upset.

Well, he definitely was incredulous. And he wasn't looking forward to having to go through all that again, but he did. However, before the doctors could open him another time, he had to take a lot of Vitamin K to make the proteins necessary for his blood to clot so his wound could heal.

There we were again for the second time around. My father-in-law was ready to attend the procedure. We had spoken with the doctors who were to perform the operation. They wheeled Fernando into the operating room, and Aurorita and I waited—and waited—and waited. Finally, my father-in-law came out and told us the procedure had been more complicated than they had expected. They had to saw one of Fernando's ribs off and ultimately take his whole kidney. Fernando had waited too long. This had been necessary. (Remember, this was in 1974, and medicine was a little different than today. Maybe the operation would have been different now.) It was good that my father-in-law had been observing the operation and agreed with the doctors' decisions. That way we wouldn't be doubting everything.

We waited some more, and finally Fernando was wheeled back to his room. And then we had to tell him what had happened that time. At least he wasn't going to need another operation, but he was left with one less rib and one less kidney.

After Fernando finally totally recovered, he had to deal with the jokes about him being a sangrón, and also jokes about God taking a rib from Adam to make Eve...

We certainly didn't see all that coming, but we still had much to thank God for. Fernando was alive and well. He could continue being a good father for Jeanette and a husband for me. Thank you, Lord.

The third big event that occurred while we were living in our house in El Pedregal didn't happen at the house, but rather while we were living in our house. My very good high school friend from Green Bay, Chris Bader, had said she'd like to visit us. Fernando was fine with that, so she came. We took her to places in Mexico City, and then my husband suggested we take a trip through a big part of Mexico. We were up for it, so the suggestion became a reality. The trip was amazing. I have always loved Mexican culture and archaeology sites, and we saw stunning, breathtaking ruins. We drove to Puebla and visited some of those 288 churches and continued on to the state of Oaxaca. It seems there are ruins everywhere there, and we visited the most well-known of them. We had a special type of hiking backpack to carry Jeanette in, and Fernando and I would take turns carrying her. Then Chris, Jeanette, Fernando, and I would go exploring. We visited the Cuilapan Monastery, marveled at the Zaachila Ruins, walked through the Lamyteco Ruins, and especially enjoyed the Monte Albán, Mitla, and Yagul Ruins. What an awe-inspiring trip for someone who loves history and ruins. Fernando and I were fortunate that we both loved history, different cultures, and, especially, ruins. And my friend Chris enjoyed the trip, too.

But we weren't done yet. Fernando kept driving south until we came to Tuxtla Gutierrez, the capital of Chiapas. He had some friends there, as he had done his "*servicio social*" there. All undergraduates in Mexico had to do some kind of servicio social, or social service, and Fernando had gone to Chiapas to do his. There he became friends with other people his age who were studying architecture. We visited with one of his friends who happened to have an American wife from St. Louis, Missouri. We all hit it off well. It was interesting to see how well his wife, Jan, had adapted to life there.

After that visit, we were back on the road to return to Mexico City. My friend Chris returned to Green Bay. Then, one day, Fernando asked me, "How would you like to move to Oaxaca or Chiapas?"

Well, to refer to the title of this selection, I didn't see that coming. I considered it, though. Both states were so different from Mexico City. Oaxaca at that time did not have a huge population. It was about 110,000 people. Tuxtla Gutierrez had about 78,000 people. Both had larger populations than Green Bay's 30,000 people when I was growing up there, but they had much less than the nine-and-a-half million people in Mexico City. That was a huge plus for me. I could probably drive by myself in those places and have a little more freedom. And those tropical plants and palm trees in Tuxtla were so different than anything I had experienced until then, so why not?

And with that another door opened to a very different life.

CHAPTER EIGHT

Yikes! What just happened?
Or
The Birth of Our
Second Daughter

"Look at my hand!" I shrieked. "It's just hanging there. I'm getting sick. I think I'm going to faint!"

"Here, cover it up with my *paleacate* (bandana), said Fernando. "Don't look at it. We'll go back and get you fixed up."

I had never broken any bone of my body, and there I was, seven months pregnant, in Chiapas, standing in a very remote area at the bottom of the Sabinal Canyon where the Río Sabinal and the Río Grijalva come together. I remember how exciting that view was—the tall trees, the bright blue sky, and the dirty, bubbly foam swirling all around where the two rivers met. And the gigantic boulders. They were my downfall, literally. As my husband, my five-year-old daughter, Jeanette, and I were hiking around those big boulders, I slipped and fell. As I was seven months pregnant, I did the most logical thing—I stuck out my arms to protect my protruding stomach. And then, looking at my hand, I started freaking out. I had broken both bones of my left wrist, and my hand just hung there. My husband and daughter were at my side, helpless. It was going to be a long trek back to the car, a long ride back to the city, and an even longer wait for a doctor.

"Let's get going," begged my husband. "I'll help you. Jeanette, you be very careful. I don't want any other accidents right now." And with that we cautiously inched our way back to the road and the car.

Getting from where we were to the car and then to the main road was another adventure. We had to walk back through that boulder strewn area, careful not to have any other catastrophe happen. Then, once we got into the car, new problems arose. The road up from the canyon was all loose gravel and our old DKW car didn't have much traction or power. All of that resulted in me—with my broken bones and my hand hanging—having to get out of the car at times and walk up that gravel road while my husband tried to get the car to drive up it. What a fiasco, but we finally made it.

And then . . .

"When will we find a doctor to see me? Are there no doctors available on a Sunday here?"

There I was, sitting on a bench in a hospital in Tuxtla Gutierrez, Chiapas, looking at my hand just dangling—the wrist bones no longer connected to my hand. It was a Sunday afternoon in 1976. There was NO ONE around. And we had already been waiting for a while. Then my husband decided to try to find our compadre, his *tocallo* (person of the same name), Fernando de la Fuente. Soon they arrived at the hospital with a doctor.

"Dr. García. Am I glad to see you!" That man was the husband of one of my good friends. My anxiety level lowered quickly. Dr. García checked out my hand, held my hand and my elbow, pulled both, and . . . SNAP. My wrist bones were back in place. I could hardly process what had just happened. And then the good doctor got someone there to put a hard plaster on my arm from my fingers all the way up to almost my armpit (with a little bend at the elbow so I would be able to function some!) And then we were off, back to reality!

One month later at the hospital . . .

"Oh, no, Doctor. This is not good. I can't even tickle my baby with this big cast on." My little María was just born—one month early. Instead of keeping my left arm in a sling while my wrist bones healed, I had just rested my arm on my pregnant belly. I guess the weight from that pushed my baby down faster, and she was born one month early, and a breech birth at that. Before we left the hospital, though, they cut the cast to just below my elbow, and I was able to take care of my precious newborn. A week later the cast was cut off entirely, and the saga of the Sabinal Canyon adventure was over.

God does exist, and I have no doubt that God was with me in that canyon. Only my husband, daughter Jeanette, and I were there. Even though it seemed like a real disaster at the time, and those broken bones were freaking me out, it could have been much worse. I could have lost my baby right there. Instead, I only broke the two bones of my wrist. We had a very challenging time getting back to the city, but we got there. It was difficult to find a doctor, but we found one, and a friend at that. María Fernanda was born breech and one month early, but she was a healthy little baby. And, finally, that horrible cast was completely cut off. God was with me, and He was in control. And I had a powerful life event to use to witness to the glory of God—and to bring me closer to Him in my need for His protection, healing, and comfort. I thank the Lord.

CHAPTER NINE

Baby Number Three

I always wanted three children of my own. I had grown up with one pretty cool brother and a much younger, but great, sister. I really thought that the number three for siblings was perfect, and I asked God to please bless me with the same, preferably daughters. Well, God was listening to my prayers. Jeanette, María, and Ana are my three darling daughters, all gifts of God for us to enjoy, guide, and protect. The birth of my baby number three also had its share of drama.

"I can't believe this is happening to me. Not now. Couldn't this have happened at least one day later?"

So, what was happening to me? Well, there I was, standing in the women's bathroom of the human resources department of the ISSSTE (*Instituto de Seguridad y Servicios Sociales de los Trabajadores del Estado*, a federal government organization in Mexico that administers part of Mexico's health care and social security systems), and my water broke. I had gone there to put in my papers for maternity leave from the *Universidad Autónoma de Chiapas* (UACH), the Autonomous University of Chiapas, where I was teaching English as a Second Language (ESOL). At that time, November of 1980, educators were granted maternity leave of one month before birth and two months after. As circumstances would have it, I was only going to get the two months after birth, as my water broke before the one month before birth began, and that was the beginning of an interesting set of events.

"Oh, my goodness. What do I do now?" Well, the obvious thing to do was to call my husband. He was by my side in the blink of an eye, and off we went to the hospital. To this day, I don't remember how or who got the required documentation done for the maternity leave. All I remember is that we went to the hospital, called my doctor, our friend Dr. Humberto Camacho, and waited for his diagnosis. According to him, Ana wasn't ready to enter this world yet, so he put me on bed rest. Oh no.

So, bed rest it was. My neighbor Rosita Rincón had wanted to give me a baby shower and decided to go through with it. She did all the preparations, invited my friends, and held the baby shower at my house. All the guests had arrived. I was in my bedroom for the bed rest, and the baby shower was in full bloom, when, suddenly, I started to feel contractions. My husband called Doctor Camacho again. He was at the house in a flash. He listened to the baby's heartbeat. Other excited guests did, too. Then it was time to get to the hospital. My baby was ready. (And my friends finished the baby shower without me.)

"Ay ay ay. Humberto, you better get ready. These contractions are really strong!" Can you believe it? There were my husband and my doctor sitting on the little bed next to mine shooting the breeze. Well, the doctor jumped up, checked me out, and said, "You better wait. I have to get my gown on and get scrubbed in."

It wasn't long after that and my third daughter, Ana, was born. Another little bundle of joy. And I had two months to dedicate myself to her and Jeanette and María before going back to teaching ESOL at the UACH.

An add-on to this: One day when my neighbor Rosita was visiting me, she said she thought my eyes looked quite yellow, and that I should go get that checked out, so I did. I was so surprised when I was told I had hepatitis. The jaundiced eyes were the give-away. I was told I probably contracted it in the hospital when I had Ana. That resulted in an interesting situation. It was contagious, so I had to stay in my bedroom by myself. I was served my food on disposable plates and utensils. Nobody wanted to be by me—not even my husband. Only my neighbor would come and sit by me sometimes. And my baby? My Godsend of a neighbor, Rosita, took care of her until I was able to.

Many more "God moments" here. I have no doubt that God is present in my life and in all our lives. We just need to learn how to recognize and appreciate all that He does for us.

CHAPTER TEN

Education in Tuxtla

I was blessed with the parents I had and a great place to grow up—and also a great time to grow up. I thank the Lord every day for that. Yes, I'm one of those people who can say I walked more than a mile to school rain or shine, blistering, humid heat, or freezing cold with huge snow drifts. It was actually kind of exciting. I loved it. At that time, kids could be kids without the fear of so many terrible dangers that children today could face. It was a different time in so many ways. However, I must say, my daughters were also blessed to be brought up in Tuxtla Gutierrez, Chiapas, Mexico, at the time they lived there. Even though it was the capital of the state, it had the air of a small town, and parents knew the parents of their children's friends. And children could really enjoy their childhood. I am writing this part of our story now, many years later, and sadly, that is not the case anymore. That city—and a good part of Mexico- is a very dangerous place to live nowadays.

I pray that my daughters feel as positive about their childhood as I do about mine. I think they do. They are products of two worlds: Mexico and the United States. They appreciate the culture of where they grew up, as well as the culture here in the United States, where they live now, which will be covered later.

As far as their early education, all three of my daughters attended the *Colegio de Niñas*, or Girls' School, that was run by the nuns. My daughter Jeanette was in a class of fifty-five students. . That was in the third grade, a very difficult, important year for students. I don't know how those Catholic Sisters were able to control all those young girls, but they sure did. And Jeanette received an excellent education. Before that, she had been in an outstanding public school in the same city, but we had to take her out due to the teacher strikes. The Colegio de Niñas proved to be a great move for her, though. She thrived there. However, for my other two daughters…

"Your daughter was writing on her friend's leg." There I was with my daughter in Sister Ceci's office listening to the nun accuse my daughter María of doing such a terrible thing. I had the hardest time keeping a straight face. If that was the worst she did, I could live with that.

"Your daughter broke one of our big *macetas* (flowerpots) when she was chasing another girl. That flowerpot needs to be replaced." That was the *Madre Directora* (principal) in a different meeting, also discussing my daughter María.

"Ouch. That hurt!" That was my daughter Ana after her second-grade teacher hit her on the head with a wooden pointer. And it broke. How did she deserve such physical torture? She had gone to the bathroom, and when she returned, her teacher, a Catholic Sister, asked her why she had taken such a long time. Ana responded nonchalantly just that—that she had gone to the bathroom. The Sister got upset and said my daughter was being disrespectful and followed up with the strike. And then she told Ana that she owed her a new pointer. When my daughter got home, she told me the story of how she was indignant that her teacher had treated her like that. Well, I didn't want to cause any unnecessary friction between her and the school, so, as I was teaching at the Instituto Bicultural at that time, I had a metal expandable pointer, and I sent that with my daughter to assuage the Sister's ire.

I guess I had two quite uncouth daughters. They also did get a high-quality education there, however, even though they were so "wild."

And I was their English teacher. At that time, I was teaching at the *Instituto Bicultural*, a school sponsored by the United States Department of Agriculture for the children of the Americans who were working in the area to eradicate the *gusano barrenador*, or screwworm. This plague had been eradicated down to the southern border of the United States with Mexico. The plan then was to create an American community on the southern border of Mexico with Guatemala to eradicate the screwworm all the way down to that locale. The American adults would work on sterilizing the flies so they would not lay their eggs in the wounds of animals, resulting in the transformation of the eggs into the screwworms that would eventually kill the animals by feeding off the open wounds. Their children attended the school established for them, the Instituto Bicultural, which was supposed to be composed of half Mexican children and the other half children of the American employees. The purpose was to enhance the understanding of all involved in the different cultures and languages. The teachers were all Americans, and I was fortunate enough to be accepted as one of them. I must say that school never lacked anything, and all the children thrived. I was able to use their books to teach my daughters English at our home, too.

And that I did. I would talk mostly English to my daughters, while my husband and most everybody else would speak Spanish to them. My daughters would come up with some interesting sentences like, "*Mira la ball*," ("Look at the ball."), or "*Yo quiero pasgetti*" ("I want spaghetti."), as they were code-switching without realizing it. My middle daughter, María, was the most *rebelde* (rebellious). When we'd go up to Wisconsin to visit my parents, I needed my daughters to speak English, as my parents, brother, and sister didn't speak Spanish. Well, little María, who was probably about five years old at that time, would say, "*Yo no hablo ENGLISH!*" ("I don't speak English!"), totally emphasizing the word English. That would crack us up, but it didn't help the communication between her and her grandparents.

My oldest daughter learned English quite well, and she decided she wanted to earn some money for herself by teaching her friends English. She had watched me teach a group of Mexican girlfriends English at our house and figured she could do that. Well, her daddy supported her wishes and got about eight little school desks with tables connected to them from a CAPFCE (*Comité Administrador del Programa Federal de Constucción de Escuelas*) school he was renovating. At that time, he was an architect working for the CAPFCE and was able to get the chairs for her. We put them outside on our porch, and the little girls would sit there while Jeanette would give them their lessons. Jeanette was quite a pill, though. She would wait until about ten minutes before the class was about to start, and then she'd come to me and ask, "What should I teach today?" I would always get upset that she would wait until the last minute, but it's amazing how well she could teach those classes even without preparation. She'd have them dancing around singing "Ring Around the Rosy," and all kinds of fun things. She was about twelve at that time and used her earnings as spending money when we'd go up to the States to visit.

As far as teaching at the Instituto Bicultural, the situation was definitely different than teaching in the United States. The school covered kindergarten through eighth grade. It only had about sixty students at a time, so the classes were small. The interesting part was that I had English grades three, four, and five all at the same time. All in the same hour. And then I had grades six, seven, and eight all at the same time in another class. That class was the most challenging. The sixth graders were so much more immature than the seventh and eighth graders, and the seventh and eighth graders could cover much more difficult material. I enjoyed teaching these classes, though, and a few years later, one of my students told me that he didn't have to study much of anything in his English classes in ninth grade back in the States because we had covered it all—even some of the stories—in my classes in Mexico.

Along with the English classes, I also taught Spanish and music. We didn't have any music books, so I gathered songs from the piano music I had at my house and got them printed up and bound into a great songbook. I had a lot of children's songs that I played on my piano at home while my own children and I sang, and those songs came in handy.

American history was my favorite class to teach—and my very favorite project was when we were studying the American Indians. I had my seventh- and eighth-grade students bring shovels and buckets to school. Then, on the designated day, we all walked across the big field in front of the school and down to the Sabinal River. There, I had the students dig up dirt and almost fill their buckets. Then we carried all that heavy dirt back to the school. I had typed up little slips of paper with quotes from famous American Indians about how they respected the earth, animals, and all of nature. The next day, they took their buckets, dumped the dirt in the middle of the classroom (the desks had been moved to the sides), sat on the floor in a big circle around the big pile of dirt, lit candles, and took turns reading the quotes I had typed. As each student read a quote, s/he would take a bowlful of the dirt away from the pile and put it in the buckets behind them. As the pile of dirt was dwindling, I would remind them that that is what the settlers that had come from the Old World did to the American Indians—they took their land away from them. It was so refreshing to see how somber the students were as they participated in the activity.

It really is sad how now in the United States those in charge are so concerned about test scores and restrict the time teachers can take to do innovative activities in the classroom.

CHAPTER ELEVEN

Times to Pray and Times to Play

As I've told you, I was in Wisconsin, and after I got married, I moved from the northern border of the United States to Mexico City (about 2,250 miles away). Shortly after that my parents decided to move south to avoid the harsh winters in Green Bay and settled in El Paso, Texas. Soon after that, my husband wanted us to move from Mexico City to Tuxtla Gutierrez, Chiapas, on the southern border of Mexico (about 1,660 miles from El Paso to Tuxtla). I guess he wanted to maintain his distance.

But we did enjoy living in Tuxtla. Life was different there, but in good ways. One way concerned our ability to celebrate God in a variety of forms.

Yes, it's "the wheel of God." That's what I would hear. (But what was really being said was, "It's the will of God.") Because of the rather large American community due to the screwworm program, an ordained Baptist minister, Milton Howard, who was serving as a missionary in the area, offered to give nondenominational services in his house on Sunday mornings. His wife Claudia would bake delicious cookies, which she shared with the people who attended. These missionaries were from the deep South in the United States and had pronounced accents. I found the accents quite enjoyable. And my young daughters found the homemade cookies a special treat. It was great to celebrate God in English in the company of other believers. It was so wonderful of this devoted couple to open their house to us. What a blessing to us all. God is good.

I would also take my daughters to the Mexican churches in the city. (My husband said he'd only go to church for baptisms, weddings, and funerals, so it was up to me.) I was a Lutheran all my life, and I noted that the Catholic services resembled our Lutheran services in many ways. I just wouldn't say the parts I didn't really agree with.

"Madre, sería posible que yo tomara comunión en la iglesia?" ("Could I have permission to take communion in the Catholic church?") I asked the Madre Directora (principal) of the Catholic girls' school my daughters were attending. I told her I found the Catholic service very similar to the Lutheran one I had been brought up on. I told her that our creed, which I had in the Lutheran hymnal, was almost the same as theirs. I just didn't feel comfortable taking communion in the Catholic church without discussing this with someone of authority. Many people knew I wasn't Catholic, and I didn't want to be disrespectful to the worshippers, but I really did miss not taking the holy communion. The Madre Directora told me to take her the hymnal so she could see it. I did.

"OK, *usted puede tomar comunión, pero la va a estar tomando como Luterana."* ("You can take communion, but you will be taking it as a Lutheran.") Well, that was fine with me. I felt much better, though, getting permission.

My faith was an integral part of my life, and I raised my daughters to have a strong faith, too. That wasn't difficult to do in Tuxtla, as that city—like most of Mexico—was predominantly a Catholic belief-based population. My daughters participated in fun youth group meetings, often in the racquetball court in our backyard. Some parents helped, and everybody felt strong ties to God and to each other.

My daughters' faith was the foundation of their lives as they grew up in Mexico. My grandparents instilled a strong faith in my parents, which was then instilled in my brother, sister, and me by them. I did everything I could to continue this with my own children, and I'm so pleased to say that they are also doing what they can to foster a strong faith in their offspring. That's five generations there—and I'm sure the generations before my grandparents taught their children the importance of God in their lives, also. It's heartening to know that parents can definitely have very positive influences in their children's lives.

As parents, we have real power over the future of our children. There is nothing like spending undistracted time dedicated to our children, while also supervising, or at least being aware of their activities, their friends, and their acquaintances, along with asking God for guidance, blessings, and protection. We are our children's compass, and we must do all we can to point them in the right direction. Sadly, sometimes society intervenes, and maybe we don't even recognize problems our children have, or we don't understand how to deal with them until it is too late. God help us!

Besides our times to pray and celebrate God, we also had plenty of opportunities to play—to enjoy our lives in Tuxtla. One healthy pastime we had as a family was to go to our *ranchito* (little ranch). It was about a half-hour drive from the outskirts of Tuxtla on the way to the old airport. Fernando built a "tiny home" on the property for the essentials. We had two horses—one for Jeanette and one for María. We had one cow—that I don't remember anybody milking—guinea hens, geese, a pheasant, and chickens. Fernando had excavated a big area and cemented it in for a pool, but he had to bring water in from the city. He had dug for a well, but there wasn't much water. This ranchito of ours became a place our friends and their children loved to go to, too. There was a little creek nearby that the teenagers would hike to. We would shoot at tin can targets and play baseball (Fer's friends called him *Piñatero*, because he'd swing at any ball pitched to him, even the very high balls, just as children swing at piñatas at parties.). María Fernanda loved to swing and twist around in the hammock. We'd build *fogatas* (bonfires) and sing songs and tell stories. Our friends of all ages remember those times fondly. Those were perfect opportunities to spend time with good company and appreciate the beauty of God's creation as we'd admire the countryside and marvel at the grandeur of the sunsets in the evenings. The magnificence of God is everywhere. We just need to take the time from the hustle and bustle of our busy lives to recognize it.

Just as we enjoyed our ranchito and had many animals there, we also had our share of animals at our house in the city, and we had many opportunities to "play" with them. We had two loving cocker spaniels, Dumbo (because of his big ears) and *Pecas* (because he looked like he had a lot of freckles). Pecas was given to Jeanette when it was a very young puppy. She had to feed it about every three hours at first. There she had me, also, feeding my "grand dog" when she couldn't. When it grew up, it loved to jump up on our round metal table that was positioned on our porch right outside the kitchen window. It loved to watch us cooking and cleaning up, and we loved to watch it watch us.

"Guys, Pecas is foaming at the mouth and having a hard time walking."

It was very early one morning. I had heard Pecas barking a lot. Then I opened the door from the family room to the porch, and there was Pecas. I didn't know what was happening. Everyone else darted out quickly. My husband said it looked like our dog had been poisoned.

"Give him some milk. See if he can drink it."

It was so sad to watch Pecas struggle. Fernando took Jeanette to get a vet, but it was too late. She and her boyfriend ended up taking Pecas to a place out in the country for his final resting place. We found out that

Pecas had been poisoned by a bufo toad, a gigantic poisonous toad native to South and Central America (they are also in Florida). We didn't even know those toads existed until then. I think that toad was hiding in our bamboo plants that lined the wall outside our house. After Pecas died, I did find a few more of those toads outside by our plants. I would open our gate to the street and bat them out with a broom, screaming all the while.

And we had many more pets.

"*Comadre, ese chihuahua no es tan feo!*" ("That chihuahua isn't that ugly!") Our good friends Marta and Guillermo lived out in the country in Berriozabal and had a multitude of chihuahuas. I would always say that I thought they were ugly, with their bugged-out eyes, but that little chihuahua was kind of cute. Well, Marta said we could have it and gave it to María. María named him Timmy because he was *tímido* (timid) and shaking a lot—probably from fear of us. María even trained him, and we took him to a number of dog shows. He won a lot of diplomas and ribbons, but once in a while he would have his own mind and refuse to budge when prodded to walk. That was quite a sight to see poor María dragging him along.

We ended up having quite a few chihuahuas. We were also given *Cosita* (Little Thing), that became Timmy's wife, and they had Packer, their baby. Packer later died of worms. I'll never forget how those worms looked on the cement outside. Yuck. And Packer was one of María's favorite dogs. It's so difficult to deal with death, but the deaths of these beloved animals can help prepare people for times when humans they love die.

"Your macaws are out in the field again." That was our neighbor. We had two gorgeous macaws, *Chavo* and *Chava* (Boy and Girl). Their wings were clipped, and they couldn't go much farther than the roof over our library. They loved to go up there and sun themselves, though, and once in a while, they would end up in the vacant lot next door to us. Finally, Fernando gave them to a friend of ours who made them a big, beautiful, ornate cage.

"That bird cannot be walking all around our house like that. It's making a mess wherever it goes." That was me saying the toucan my husband brought home could not be roaming wild in our house. Well, we compromised, and the toucan ended up in our daughters' bathroom when the girls were not watching it. That ended up being a fatal decision, as it fell ill and also died. How sad. It was a beautiful bird, but it needed to be free.

Another death that was on our hands was a bright green parrot with a black tongue. It could say a few words, and my daughters were fascinated with it. We had it in a cage outside on our porch. With time, they didn't pay much attention to it. And then someone hung it out by the swing set. Well, one day somebody noticed it was no longer sitting on its perch. It had died. It died *de tristeza* (of sadness), and that makes me sad to this day.

All those deaths were difficult for us to handle. They definitely made us aware of our own mortality. And they provided opportunities to discuss how blessed we are to have our faith in God and know that Jesus died to redeem us of our sins so that we may live again—a better life with Him and our loved ones in Heaven. As we enjoy life, with tragedies like these, we are drawn back to our need to stay close to God and appreciate what he does for us. Our times to play often also result in times to pray. They are not mutually exclusive.

"Oh my God. You must see this. I think we have all the bees in our city right outside our door." Sure enough. There were swarms of honeybees outside. My husband had tried his luck as a beekeeper for a time. He had built wooden box hives with the necessary frames coated with beeswax and bought manual metal bee smokers and beekeeping hoods with fencing veils. The "beehives" were placed in our ranchito. We all tried our hand at "inspecting" those boxes. There you had us wearing long sleeves, no shiny jewelry (so as not to attract the bees), hoods with netting (to protect our faces) and pumping the smokers to calm the bees so we could check on how the honey was being produced. We learned a lot about the art of beekeeping. However, this time Fernando and our compadre Paco Gómez were a bit careless. They had gone to the ranchito, gotten bee frames filled with honey, and put them in a big metal tub to bring it all back to our house. They had left that metal tub on our ping pong table on the porch and gone inside the house. Hours later, someone went outside for something and heard all the buzzing and saw all the swarms of bees. Paco and Fernando hurried to move the tub—I don't even remember where to. What I do remember is how Paco's face ended up so swollen he was hardly recognizable. (I guess I exaggerate a little bit, but it was immensely swollen.) He was allergic to bees. That attempt to get rid of the bees could have been fatal. Thank God Paco was able to recover.

More excitement on another day:

"Mom. I think someone is drowning!" My little María was shouting that as she was running toward us. Sure enough, there was a person who, by that time, was down towards the bottom of the deep end of the Olympic-sized pool of the Club Los Sabinos where I would take my daughters. Someone else heard her and jumped into action to get the person out. María had advised us in the nick of time, and that person was saved. Thank the Lord.

Yes, the Club Los Sabinos was a fun place to go when my daughters were growing up. My very good friend Jan de La Fuente (the person I met when my husband took my childhood friend Chris Bader and me on that aforementioned first trip to Chiapas) would take her two sons, Fernando and Mark, about the same ages as my daughters, also, and our kids enjoyed swimming, playing tennis, playing ping pong, basketball, and bowling together. Yes, bowling. Jan and her sons and my daughters and I loved to go bowling there. But this bowling was very unique. The Club had two "manual bowling alleys." We would throw the bowling balls. A little Mexican guy would jump off his perch above the pin area and get the downed pins out of the way. He'd then roll the ball back to us for the second throw and jump back up on his perch and wait. Once the pins fell on the second throw, he'd roll the ball back to us. Then, he'd position the bowling pins in the rack above and lower the rack with a rope to reset the ten pins for the next bowler. That guy got a workout. And a nice tip! And we all had some great times honing our bowling skills. My daughter Ana remembers the little guy's feet dangling as he sat there and waited for the balls to hit the pins and thought he was really brave. She would say, "I wouldn't want to do that!"

One thing my oldest daughter, Jeanette, didn't want to have anything to do with was exploring the many ruins in the state of Chiapas when she was young. Throughout my life I have loved traveling and, luckily, my husband did, too. We took many trips all around Mexico during our time together. Fernando was proud of his country and always reveled in showing it off. Our daughters benefited from all the traveling, too. I will never forget, however, what a pill Jeanette was one time when she was little. We had finally gotten around to visiting the ruins of Chichén Itzá, in the state of Yucatán. I had always wanted to go there. Well, that time, Jeanette was having none of it. She shouted out, "*Yo no quiero ver esas piedras!*" ("I don't want to see those rocks!") Needless to say, I wasn't very happy about that.

Many years later, after Jeanette completed her studies in Mexico, she moved up to the United States and stayed with my parents to further her education. She studied interior design and graduated with straight A's. I was proud of her accomplishments, as she was taking all her classes in English. Back in Tuxtla, María, Ana, and I started taking German classes in the evenings at the Cosmolingua school. Our teacher, Martin, was from Germany, and he gave great classes, and it was fun—and challenging—to learn that language together as a family. The highlight of those classes was an exciting bus trip a big group of us took to tour around Chiapas trying to speak German as much as we could while traveling.

My daughters, my husband, and I did many fun things together as a family and, as with my Mexican friends, I also had opportunities to enjoy moments with my American friends. As mentioned earlier, there were many Americans in Tuxtla Gutierrez when I lived there. Some, like Jan and me, were married to Mexican citizens. Jan and I were very close friends. We had so much in common. We were both from the United States. We were both teachers. She also taught at the Instituto Bicultural for a while. Both our husbands' names were Fernando. Both were architects, and they were good friends, too. We have many fond memories of our families doing things together. And Jan and I did many things with the Americans that were there with the screwworm program.

"What is the strongest organ in the human body?" That was an unforgettable question in our Trivial Pursuit game. As my friend Nancy asked the question, she stuck out her tongue. Gosh, I wonder what it could be. It was the tongue, according to the Trivial Pursuit card, and we got quite a kick out of it. There were many more wild questions in that game, too. I think we learned a lot of useless, but fun information.

Yes, we did play Trivial Pursuit. We would get together once a week at each other's houses to play the game and have fun. I was lucky that at the time I lived in Tuxtla the US government program was in full force and there was such a big American community. I had my American friends, my Mexican friends, and my wonderful family. My life was complete.

Family Traditions and Celebrations

This is a fun section about family traditions and celebrations. As previously stated, my goal is to leave a legacy for you, my family, through our stories that will enable you to understand your roots, preserve memories, and find peace and happiness in your lives. At the same time, I want to be a witness to God for you and everyone else reading this. This book is a testament to the power of faith and family. Family is a gift from God, and it is to be treasured and nurtured. I would like each one of you reading this to consider these questions for your family: "What can I leave you?" "How will you remember me?" "How will I have influenced your thoughts and actions?" "What's really important in life?" Our response to these questions will influence generations to come.

Some of our family traditions and celebrations here are an expression of our faith, as you will see in the selections of *La Rosca de Reyes* (the King's Bread) and *El Día de los Muertos* (the Day of the Dead). As you read about these, you may also learn some interesting facts. Other traditions and celebrations are just fun ways to create memories and strong family bonds. May our stories inspire you to create your own memories.

CHAPTER TWELVE
What's a Rosca de Reyes?

"I got a baby!" one of the children exclaimed happily.

"I want a baby!" shouted another.

The adults were just as enthused as the children. Everyone was crowding around the Rosca de Reyes, watching intently.

"Remember, you need to cut your own piece."

What is going on here? What baby? Piece of what? Well, it's a baby Jesus hidden in a cake. This is part of the Catholic celebration of the Rosca de Reyes, or King's Bread or Ring, also known as King's Cake. It is a very unique sweet cake made in the shape of a circle or an oblong representing, for some people, the crown of the King Of Kings (Jesus, the King of the Jews) and His everlasting love, and for others, the crowns and the jewels of the *Reyes Magos* (the Three Kings, or Wise Men), Melchor, Gaspar, and Baltazar, who had gone in search of the baby Jesus of Nazareth by following the bright North Star until they reached Mary, Joseph, and Jesus in Bethlehem. (See the complete story in the Bible in Matthew Chapter 2.)

The cake is decorated with red, green, brown, and even yellow candied fruits of cherries, melons, figs, and possibly pineapples, with wide strips of a streusel kind of topping between the fruits. These candied fruits also represent the jewels of the kings or the gifts of the kings for the baby Jesus.

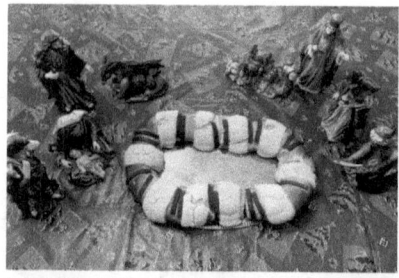

The most exciting part of the rosca is the little plastic baby Jesus—or probably three baby Jesuses—baked into the cake. They represent the newborn Christ child hiding from the troops sent by King Herod to kill all the males two years old and under to eliminate this infant, whom Herod feared, as he had been told by those three kings that Jesus would be the King of the Jews.

At the party, each person must cut his or her own piece of the cake to see if s/he gets a baby. If a person gets a baby Jesus, it's good luck, but it also means that then that lucky person is a symbolic godparent and is supposed to offer a party of tamales and hot chocolate or *atole* (a hot corn and masa drink) on February second, which is the *Día de la Candelaria*, or Candlemas. This religious day is when Jesus was taken to the temple to be blessed. Some people take this very seriously and get a special porcelain Jesus doll and dress it up in great finery and sit it on a little wooden chair and call the party the *Sentada del niño* or sitting of the boy. I only really saw this once, but it was breathtaking. They had a little procession to take the baby to an altar there at the party, and the party would begin.

The actual celebration of the Rosca de Reyes is on January 6th, which is Epiphany, considered the day the Three Wise Men arrived to see the baby Jesus. At one time, that is when the Mexican (and some European) children would get their Christmas presents, instead of on December 25th, but now most everybody gets the presents in December. However, because this celebration of the Rosca de Reyes is so important, most people who celebrate this wait until after January 6th to take down all the Christmas decorations.

"Ok, I need three volunteers to take the three kings over to the table where Mary, Joseph, Jesus, the shepherds, and the animals are gathered." (Actually, this takes place before the cutting of the cake.)

If there are children, I let them take the beautiful ceramic figures and place them carefully where they think the kings should be. If there are no children, the adults are eager to comply. It's so inspiring to watch these individuals do this with such reverence. It gives me goosebumps every time. And I know everybody at the get-together feels the same way. Once this is done, there is a discussion about what we are doing, why, and the symbolism of everything.

"Great. Now it's time for the rosca and the hot chocolate. Who is going to cut the first piece?" And the celebration proceeds.

For at least forty years I have invited friends and relatives to my house, both in Mexico and in Texas, to celebrate the arrival of the Three Wise Men to see the baby Jesus with a Rosca de Reyes. It is a perfect opportunity to witness to my Lord Jesus, and all who attend, adults and children alike, love to celebrate this moment together. Some of my friends who have moved away are continuing this celebration with their own families in other places. This is an ideal opportunity for you to profess your faith—and maybe start a fun family tradition, too.

(Though I did mention that this rosca is a unique cake, I noticed that people do make a similar cake in some places in the United States, especially New Orleans, to celebrate Mardi Gras.)

CHAPTER THIRTEEN

Halloween

"Trick-or-treat. Smell my feet. Give me something good to eat."

Trick-or-treating in Wisconsin in the 1950s was a carefree time when we didn't have to worry about our safety on the streets or people sabotaging the candy we were given, as people do have to worry about now. For us, Halloween was a fun, exciting holiday. All we cared about was getting all that delicious candy. And that we did. Bags and bags of candy. I have always especially loved chocolates, and it wasn't below my dignity to raid my brother's bags to get my favorites. And he didn't really care. He loved to go trick-or-treating, but he didn't have a sweet tooth like I did, so he graciously shared his treasure with me.

We never really learned about the history of Halloween, and we really didn't care. I didn't learn Halloween's history until I lived in Tuxtla Gutierrez, Chiapas, Mexico, and was teaching ESOL at the *Universidad Autónoma de Chiapas* (UACH) there. Most of us teaching ESOL were Americans hired specifically to teach Mexican students standard English so they could be successful in the pursuit of their careers, and we always collaborated to create lessons we could all use. Just as we celebrated January sixth with a Rosca de Reyes with our students, we taught them the history of Halloween. Pedagogically, taking advantage of these special days gave life to our classes and provided rich opportunities to introduce meaningful vocabulary into our students' lexicons. When I later taught elementary and junior high English (along with

Spanish, American History, and even music) at the Instituto Bicultural there in Tuxtla, a school sponsored by the US government, I continued to teach those young students the history of Halloween. After I moved back to the United States, I included teaching this Halloween history in my classes for my ESOL students at Burges High School. It's kind of fun to understand why we do the things we do.

So, what about the history of Halloween? Unlike the celebration of the Rosca de Reyes, Halloween is not a religious celebration. On the contrary, it is a pagan celebration that was first celebrated by the Celts in Ireland, Great Britain, and France, and later extended to other European countries. The Celtic celebration was called Samhain (pronounced sow-win), and took place around the end of October, when they harvested their crops to prepare for winter. That was then the end of one year and the beginning of a new one. "The Celts believed that at the time of Samhain, more so than any other time of the year, the ghosts of the dead were able to mingle with the living, because at Samhain the souls of those who had died during the year traveled into the otherworld."[1] The Celts wanted their dead to come back and visit them, and they built big bonfires to show them the way. They left food and drink for the deceased to enjoy. However, these Celts did not want the dead to stay, so they made costumes to wear to scare the dead out of their villages when the celebration was over. They wore masks so the ghosts wouldn't recognize them. Once the ghosts had left, it was time for the Celtic new year to begin.

This use of costumes and masks by the Celts to disguise who they were gave rise to the popular tradition now of pretending to be someone else. At first, the costumes were scarier, as their original intent was to frighten spirits away. With time, costumes have evolved into almost anything, even for our pets. How about a Super Dog, anybody? And just as the Celts left food and drink for their departed, people nowadays receiving the trick-or-treaters are expected to provide treats for the children so they will leave. The trick part of trick-or-treat is what could happen if treats are not dispensed. The date of October 31st correlates with the Celtics' special end of their year observances.

As for the carving of pumpkins, I used to do that as a child. Then I carved pumpkins with my children, and now a third generation—my grandchildren—also love to demonstrate their creative skills by carving ingenious designs on their pumpkins. So, why carve pumpkins for Halloween? That custom came from a very old legend about a bad man named Jack who liked to play tricks on people. Well, one day he played a trick on the devil, and the devil did not like that. When Jack died, he tried to go up to Heaven, and he was not allowed in because of his behavior. Then, he tried to enter Hell, and the devil remembered how Jack had tricked him, so he wouldn't allow Jack into Hell, either. Jack asked the devil to have mercy on him. The devil grabbed a piece of burning coal and threw it to Jack. Jack caught it, but he couldn't hold it because the coal was too hot, so he grabbed a turnip from the ground and stuck the coal inside. That gave Jack a light to facilitate his travels, and he is still flying around trying to find a resting place. A turnip is smaller, not as commonplace, and harder to carve than a pumpkin, so it was eventually replaced with a pumpkin to make bigger lanterns for poor Jack.

The question is, how did all these activities become popular in the United States? These Celtic celebrations were brought to the United States by the Irish immigrants who left Ireland during and after the Irish Potato Famine of 1845. Potatoes were a huge part of the Irish economy, and when a devastating mold destroyed the potato crops, the poor people's staple food, many of the Irish were dying of starvation. "Before it ended in 1852, the Potato Famine resulted in the death of roughly one million Irish from starvation and related causes, with at least another million forced to leave their homeland as refugees."[2] When these refugees settled in the United States, they brought their customs with them. Halloween celebrations were some of these customs, and they were enthusiastically adopted by the children in the new land.

When celebrating Halloween in Tuxtla Gutierrez, as the Instituto Bicultural was financed by the United States Department of Agriculture, we had a big budget, so we were able to give our students a great Halloween experience, something they may not have enjoyed otherwise. The students were encouraged to use their imaginations to create their costumes, and they came up with some very original ones. We also we held contests for the scariest, the cutest, the funniest, the most original, and whatever category we could think of. My all-time favorite was a child who had blown up a number of purple balloons and had his mom pin them all over him, and he went as a bunch of grapes. He really looked cute. I don't remember if he was ever able to sit down, though.

Continuing the celebrations, we would have games such as wrap the mummy, bobbing for apples, eat a complete donut of those hanging on a string on a pole in front of you, finish eating a marshmallow that is hanging on a string in your mouth without using your hands (hard to do without gagging), and many more. Sometimes, the students would carve pumpkins, too. Halloween was always a special day for those students.

Since my youngest daughter, Ana, has a birthday on November 4th, it only made sense to have a fun Halloween party for her and her guests, too. Sometimes they would dress in costumes and play all those games mentioned above at our house, too.

As far as trick-or-treating, that was not such a common practice in Chiapas when we lived there. However, as with many customs from other places, it was beginning to be absorbed into the children's celebrations in some areas of this state, too. It was changed a bit, though, in Chiapas, in a strange way. People have told me they have not heard of this in other places in Mexico, so it may have been a strange, quirky way to trick-or-treat just in this state. Some children would go to the houses and knock on the doors or gates and say, *"Calabacita, Tía"* ("Pumpkin, Auntie") referring to the festive pumpkin cut up and cooked in *piloncillo*, a hard brown sugar, and served as a very sweet treat, or *"Queremos Halloween. Queremos Halloween!"* ("We want Halloween. We want Halloween!") Then, if the people in the house gave them candy, the children would shout, *"Que viva la tía!"* ("Let live the aunt!"), or *"Que viva el tío!"* ("Let live the uncle!"), but if the people of the house would not give them any candy, the children would shout, *"Que muera la tía!"* ("Let the aunt die!") or *"Que muera el tío!"* ("Let the uncle die!") I sure didn't want them to shout that about me. I always had candy for them. (Children call adults with whom they have close friendships and relationships *tías* and *tíos* in many parts of Mexico.)

Yes, Halloween is an exciting holiday enjoyed by many people. It definitely is not a religious holiday, but it does provide many opportunities for young and old alike to spend quality time together and create positive, endearing memories.

1. "Research Guides: Halloween & Día de Muertos Resources: Introduction," Introduction - Halloween & Día de Muertos Resources - Research Guides at Library of Congress, accessed March 21, 2024, https://guides.loc.gov/halloween.

2. "Irish Potato Famine: Date, Cause & Great Hunger - History," History.com, April 11, 2023, https://www.history.com/topics/immigration/irish-potato-famine.

CHAPTER FOURTEEN

El Día de los Muertos
The Day of the Dead

You may ask, is the Día de los Muertos an extension of Halloween? The answer is an emphatic NO. As I explained in the previous section, Halloween is not a religious celebration. On the contrary, it is a pagan holiday that was first celebrated by the Celts in Ireland, Great Britain, and France. Samhain and the Día de los Muertos are similar in that in both festivities the participants want their dead to come back and visit them, they provide the dead with food and drink, and they light the way, with bonfires in the case of the Celts, and with candles for *los muertos*. However, the Celts then scared the visitors away with their disguises and masks, and a new year with new hope was to begin.

Unlike Halloween, the Día de los Muertos is not meant to be so scary, and there is so much more to it. Death is considered a part of the cycle of life, and it is seen in a very positive light. The celebration of the Día de los Muertos is considered a time to remember and honor our loved ones who have passed. It also makes us think about our own mortality and our belief in a better life in Heaven after this one, a life where we can find peace, love, and community with our loved ones, and our God and His Son, Jesus Christ.

The origin of this celebration is also very different. The Día de los Muertos, or the Day of the Dead, is a fusion of the beliefs and celebrations of the Roman Catholic Church and those of the inhabitants of present-day Mexico. All indigenous people in Mexico honored their dead. The Aztecs honored their dead for a whole month with skeletons, altars, and decorations. When the Spaniard Hernán Cortés arrived to conquer the Aztec empire in 1521, he and the other Spaniards wanted to colonize this new world, spread Christianity, and also seize their gold, silver, and other riches. As Catholics, they celebrated November first as All Saints Day, a day to venerate the saints of the church and the young children who have died. Then, November second, All Souls Day, was to celebrate all the rest who had died. The Catholic priests who arrived after these Spanish conquerors incorporated the traditions of the native inhabitants into their own church celebrations with the hope that the indigenous people would then accept Catholicism more easily. November 1st is still called All Saints Day, or *El Día de los Santos,* as well as *El Día de los Angelitos,* or Day of the Angels, to honor the children who have died, but November2nd, All Souls Day, or El Día de los Muertos, is celebrated very differently. The combination of indigenous and Catholic celebrations resulted in a very unique Día de los Muertos holiday in Mexico. (Similar celebrations developed in some other South American countries later, but when people speak of the Día de los Muertos, they are generally referring to the festivities that originated in Mexico.)

And how do we celebrate these sacred days? Death isn't sad, it's a celebration. It is one more step before we join our Lord in Heaven. And these holy days are opportunities to remember our loved ones who have passed on. We also use this time to get together with friends, family, and even strangers to honor and praise our God. There are opportunities for genuine "God moments" at every turn.

Imagine this scenario: What a beautiful sight. It's evening, and there are candles everywhere. Everyone's doors are open, and the residents are inviting friends and strangers alike inside to admire their elaborate altars, and possibly even share some *pan de muerto* (bread of the dead), tamales and *atole* (a sort of cornmeal drink that is sometimes flavored with chocolate or strawberry). The strong smell of *cempasuchil* flowers (a sort of Mexican marigold) is almost overpowering. Everyone is happy and sharing stories. A short walk away, the cemetery is bustling with people sitting alongside the graves, eating, playing the guitar or marimba, singing, and reminiscing about good times. Bright candles, crosses of all sizes, and those bright yellow-orange cempasuchil flowers are everywhere.

This was in San Andrés Mixquic on the outskirts of Mexico City, the perfect place to go to participate in traditional Day of the Dead festivities. I went there many years ago and can still see it in my mind as if I had just seen it yesterday; it was so awe-inspiring. This place and Oaxaca, Oaxaca, were the go-to places at that time. Now, even though Oaxaca is still one of the most famous sites to visit, the Day of the Dead is celebrated to the fullest almost everywhere in Mexico. Mexico City's Day of the Dead parade is renowned worldwide. And the traditions have spread to many places outside of the country—even to El Paso, Texas, where we now live.

What makes Mexico's Día de los Muertos so special is how it is celebrated. Many people love to dress up in clothes that illustrate skeletons. They paint their faces with ornate decorations, especially emphasizing their eyes. (Mattel even made Mexican Día de los Muertos Barbie dolls with eyes painted like that.) Once dressed and made up, these revelers are ready to

get together with friends, participate in parades, parties, or just walk around.

Like the special rosca bread to celebrate the Día de la Rosca de Reyes, there is a special bread for the Día de los Muertos, the *pan de muerto*, or dead man's bread. People make pan de muerto in all sizes, from the individual half-sphere size to much larger, also half-sphere pieces, which can be shared. It is a sweet bread that has its own symbolism. Just as the decorative fruits of the rosca de reyes symbolize the jewels of the Three Kings or their gifts for the baby Jesus, the pan de muerto has two cross bones on top (just like the cross bones on the symbol for pirates, although this bread does not have the skull with the bones) that represent the dead, and the sweetness of the bread conveys that death is a positive event. This bread is sold everywhere in Mexico for people to eat and to put on their altars that they create.

Another item that appears everywhere for the Día de los Muertos is the skull. There are ornate paper and posterboard cutouts of skulls and three-dimensional, hard sugar skulls, also, of all sizes. It is so fun to go to a Mexican market at this time of the year to see all these colorful skulls and look for a sugar skull that has your name on it—or a place to put your name or the name of a deceased loved-one.

In addition to the pan de muerto and the paper and sugar skulls (and now even plastic and ceramic skulls), above these market stands there are a multitude of colorful *papel picado* banners (big pieces of tissue paper with elaborate pictures related to the holiday carefully cut out of them) hanging in rows for more decoration. These banners are sold to decorate homes and offices and, especially, the altars. (More on the altars coming up.) Some people make their own papel picado by snipping out pictures much like we snip the shapes of snowflakes on white paper. But these papel picado banners are real pictures, and each little snip must be done individually to get that effect.

Some of the pictures one often sees in these papel picado banners, and in paintings, on cups, and almost everywhere, especially at this time, are famous skull and skeleton renditions of the work of the Mexican artist José Guadalupe Posada. People who have studied Mexican history know that before the Mexican Revolution, Porfirio Díaz served as president for almost forty years. During that time, the rich admired everything French and learned French, bought French things, and traveled to France, if possible. The plight of the poor was ignored. José Guadalupe Posada used his drawing ability to create great satirical pieces criticizing the conditions of the poor at that time and making fun of those French wannabees. (We're talking about the end of the 1800s and the beginning of the 1900s. If you're interested, I'm sure you'd find his drawings quite insightful and creative.) His most famous skull drawing is known as the *calavera*, or skull, Catrina. Her picture even appears on the Mexican *Lotería* game (with pictures like our object Bingo games), or at least a Catrina representing Posada's original idea of a Catrina.

The most famous way to celebrate this important day is to prepare an elaborate altar to honor our friends and relatives who have passed on. I have made altars for years in my homes, as I want my daughters to learn about their culture. They now eagerly prepare their own altars.

Here is one example. Picture this: There are green, orange, blue, and purple banners of *papel picado* hung on the wall above the altar, from the side of the table the altar was prepared on, and even possibly from the ceiling. There is a black lace tablecloth covering the altar area. On the tablecloth are *cempasuchil* flowers (or marigolds) and mums in vases, and a variety of crosses and candles interspersed with pictures of our relatives that have died, along with some of their favorite foods and drinks. Then, thought must be put into what objects to put next to each person's photos—objects that represent the person's personality, likes, activities, favorite sports teams, favorite clothes styles, hobbies, special places—anything that captures the essence of the loved one. In between all of that are many more colorfully decorated three-dimensional skulls of all sizes. And we mustn't forget to leave them a glass of water and a little salt. (These are supposedly for purification and to protect the body during its visit.) The altar is really a product of love, and as we prepare it, we relive our favorite memories of the people we honor here, and then we enjoy sharing this altar with our friends and family members. God has blessed us with so many wonderful relatives who have influenced us in their own ways. And the preparation and enjoyment of the altars provide us with the opportunity to appreciate these blessings and thank God for all He has done for us.

People prepare altars in their homes, in schools, museums, and sometimes even in workplaces to commemorate the dead. I had my students create altars at the Instituto Bicultural. Often there are also competitions for the best altars.

Yes, the celebration of the Día de los Muertos is a very special time. You might even want to pique your creativity and prepare an altar yourself next year and think of special moments you were able to spend with the people you included. Don't forget to thank God for the blessings He has bestowed on you and your loved ones. This is another activity that could become a tradition for generations to come.

(Look up El Día de los Muertos. There is a wealth of information and pictures out there. https://www.mexicodesconocido.com.mx/dia-de-muertos.html)

CHAPTER FIFTEEN

Watch Out! You're Going to Get Stoned!

My husband, my daughters, and I had left Tuxtla Gutierrez and driven the treacherous mountain road up to San Cristobal de las Casas in the highlands of Chiapas to spend the weekend in this beautiful, colonial town. It was always a treat to go there and escape the desert heat of Tuxtla. We loved visiting the *zócalo* (main square) full of people sitting along the walls of the various buildings selling typical Mexican sweets like *dulces de leche* (Mexican milk caramel candy), *mazapanes* (peanut candy marzipan style), *jamoncillo cuadrado* (soft milk candy with pecans), *camote poblano* (Mexican

sweet potato candy), *tamarindo con chile* (tamarind candy with chile), Mexican sweet breads, and so much more. So much to choose from. There were other locals selling their handmade items: crosses of every size and material, bracelets, necklaces, clay pots, woven baskets, and anything else they thought tourists might buy.

"*Por favor, cómprenme algo.*" ("Please buy something from me.") could be heard everywhere as little girls dressed in their traditional indigenous

clothing would approach, their extended hands and arms full of handmade little indigenous dolls, small, colorfully embroidered pouches, bright, woven textiles, braided bracelets, and necklaces. They asked so little money for their products. Even
so, tourists would *regatear*, or haggle, with these poor people. It's sad, as these vendors are trying so hard to get enough money together to buy what they need to subsist.

On the main plaza of the zócalo is the grand *Catedral* (Cathedral), an interesting colonial structure with ornate gold leaf decorations inside. Around the side of the Catedral is an even bigger display of regional craftmanship in an open market alongside the church. Sometimes, you can even watch the indigenous women sitting weaving cloth to make their clothing or other textiles on *a telar de cintura* (small loom connected from their waist to a tree or bench).

Two other churches here attract a significant number of visitors: La Iglesia de San Cristobalito and La Iglesia de Guadalupe. Both sit high on hills with many steps to climb to get to them. We were not going to visit them this time.

An aside: I'll never forget one time when we were here in San Cristobal with some of my husband's family.

"Señorita, podemos entrar?" ("Miss, can we enter?") This is what my husband's aunt asked the person who opened the door at *Na Bolom* (Jaguar House in Tzotzil). The person had very long, straight, black hair and was wearing a long toga-like garment. The aunt thought this person was a female. However, as her eyes focused lower, she saw hairy legs and black shoes. (Those definitely seemed out of place with the

rest of his outfit.) The man looked at her with a serious expression.

"Oh, perdón. Podemos entrar, señor?" ("Excuse me. Can we enter, sir?")

That person was a

Lacandón Indian. The Lacandones are a group of only about 1,000 Mayan people who live in the Lacandón jungle nearby. Until now, they had lived distanced from other people, thus keeping their own beliefs and customs. Now, they are starting to take advantage of tourists' interest and money and giving guided tours of their settlements, and interacting more with people who are not of their group. Casa Na Bolom is a building in San Cristobal that Gertrudis and Franz Blom set up to help support and study the Lacandón Indians. Tourists can visit this building to see pictures of these Indians in their jungle habitat, handicrafts that they make, books written about these Indians, and some of the actual Lacandón Indians themselves.

This time we stayed in our favorite place when visiting this area, a lodge-type construction a short drive outside of San Cristobal with several cabins overlooking the city. An American couple ran it. At dinner time all the guests were to meet in the main building, have a glass of wine by the fireplace, and then have a delicious, warm meal in the dining room. We always enjoyed the ambiance and meeting other travelers.

Then, it was time to return to the sweltering heat of Tuxtla Gutierrez. Before returning, however, we decided to take a detour, still in the highlands of Chiapas, to the small, remote Tzotzil Indian town of San Juan Chamula. It was a cool, hazy day.

"Look out. You're going to get stoned!" Someone was shouting that at me.

I was standing at a distance in front of the main church there. I was trying to film the church grounds, the church itself, and the Indians to the side of the church. Of course, they were wearing their native clothing. I had wanted to make videos of interesting areas, people, and customs of Chiapas for our family collection. This was back when the video recorder was gigantic. You had to hold it with one hand and almost rest it on a shoulder in order to be able to carry it around as you recorded. Well, I couldn't hide the camcorder.

Painted on bark by
M. Pastrana

And some of the Indians realized what I was doing, even though I was far away and using the zoom. They definitely did not want me to film them. Thus, the stone directed my way. With that, we decided it would be best to leave. (Supposedly, these Indians do not want their pictures taken. They think that doing so would steal their soul and that it is disrespectful to their spiritual world.)

Painted by Ana Colón

It would take us a little over an hour to get back to Tuxtla. It was even more challenging to go DOWN the mountains to return home. I was always afraid the brakes could fail, or someone could be coming around a curve and force us to crash down the mountain. My husband was driving. However, he was very tired. I could tell he was having a hard time staying awake. He had his window open and was listening to Mexican songs played loudly on the radio.

"Let me drive. You are too sleepy," I begged him.

"No, I can do it."

Well, he thought he could, but...

"YOU'RE FALLING ASLEEP!" I shouted. Yes, he was dozing off while driving down the curvy road. I shouted that so loudly that he did wake up. He finally agreed to pull over and let me drive. Well, all the way down the mountain he was wide awake and criticizing my driving. The car was not an automatic, and I definitely didn't use the clutch as well as he would have liked. I'm sure my young daughters were terrified. We did make it home safely, though. God was surely with us this trip.

But the Lord Himself goes before you and will be with you; He will never leave you nor forsake you. Do not be afraid; do not be discouraged.
Deuteronomy 31:8

CHAPTER SIXTEEN

Earthquakes and Volcanos

It was late at night. The wind burst through the window, howling as it rushed inside. The long curtains were flying horizontally in the air above us as we were lying in our bed. What a scene. I'll never forget it. And then it happened. The ground began to tremble—stronger and stronger. My husband ran to get our daughters while I scrambled to find my eyeglasses before I could go anywhere. (It's rough not to be able to see.) We ran down the long hallway, struggled to unlock the door—and then the gate, and stood outside in the street waiting for the tremors to subside. Luckily, they did subside, and we went back in and tried to sleep. In the morning we found out that some of the older, less sturdily built houses in the city had been damaged, but the bulk of the destruction had occurred in Chiapa de Corzo, a small town about 15.3 kilometers from Tuxtla. There, roofs had caved in, walls had collapsed, and great cracks had formed in walls of many buildings. We felt so bad for those people.

Another time, when I was teaching ESOL at the Universidad Autónoma de Chiapas, all my English students and I were sitting in the classroom on the second floor when the floor began to shake. We all looked at each other, wondering what to do. Then we all beelined for the hallway and the stairs. Just as we arrived at the stairs, the shaking stopped. We just looked at each other sheepishly and went back and continued nervously with the class. Thank the Lord nothing worse had happened.

Other, similar instances occur occasionally. Mexico has its share of earthquakes, some of them very destructive, with many killed and injured, causing a lot of anxiety. The earth tremors are not to be taken lightly.

And Then the Volcano…

It was March 29, 1982. I was standing in our yard watering the bushes. It was about 10 a.m. It had been a delightful, sunny day. However, just like that it seemed to start snowing—and we lived in the tropics. What was going on? The longer I stood there, the more the sky filled with this "snow." And the sky started to darken—at 10 a.m. Upon investigation, we found out that the Chichonal Volcano had erupted the day before, and the ash was arriving in Tuxtla. I hadn't even heard of that volcano until then.

The Chichonal Volcano, also known as El Chichón, is located in Francisco León in northwestern Chiapas, about 162 kilometers from where we were. Later, we found out that at least 1,900 people living near the volcano had been killed, and a great amount of sulfur dioxide— "almost 7 to 10 million tons, or roughly seven times that of the equivalently sized St. Helens eruption" (https://www.wired.com) had been released into the atmosphere. The news programs were showing pictures of buildings near the volcano with no roofs remaining and almost completely covered with ash. We were all flabbergasted.

"We need to get someone to sweep the ash off the roof. That ash is heavy. It will make the roof cave in."

"We can't run our air conditioner. It would bring that air inside, and that air is corrosive."

"We shouldn't drive our car, either. That air will corrode everything."

"So, all we can use is this floor fan? It's so hot."

"We can't stay here. We shouldn't even be breathing this air."

And with that my husband Fernando, my daughters Jeanette, María, and Ana, and I were off to Mexico City, 842 kilometers away, as refugees seeking solace with Kate and Jorge Perez Montes de Oca, my husband's sister, and her husband. As we drove, it continued "snowing" all the way to Oaxaca, Oaxaca, about 500 kilometers away. That was crazy. We did have a wonderful visit with Kate and Jorge in Mexico City, though.

We were some of the lucky people who were able to escape the volcano aftermath, thank God.

Where is God in all this? Why does God allow natural disasters? Why does God allow suffering? God did not promise us a perfect life without problems, but He promised to walk alongside us through our dark times. God is our anchor, our steady support, and we are never alone.

CHAPTER SEVENTEEN

Good-bye, My Dear Friend, Until We Meet Again

"Do we have everything we need? Let's check and make sure. Rope, flash-lights, matches, food, water, phones, cameras, a first aid kit, plastic bags…

Are we missing anything? Is everybody here? Let's go."

My daughter Jeanette, my precious friend Marilu's son Jose Alberto, and a group of their friends were preparing for an eventful day explor-ing a cave off the road on the way to Don Ventura outside of Tuxtla Gutierrez, Chiapas, Mexico. The excitement in the air was palpable. And it was time to take off. My *comadre*[1] Marilu and I were going to take them to their destination. We each had a big Volkswagen van and had agreed to take these explorers where they wanted to go, drop them off, and pick them up at the time they had requested for that afternoon. The friends' parents knew of this adventure and were happy to let them participate.

We had to climb up a mountain to get to the cave. The winding road was treacherous. I told Marilu I would follow her, as I don't like to drive, and she could lead the way. I remembered the song, "The Long and Winding Road," of which only the title applied to our trip, but that's what this felt like. The teenagers were all wound up, talking excitedly about their highly anticipated adventure.

And then we were there. The friends hopped out of the vans, got their gear, crossed the road, and disappeared into the foliage after being reminded of the pick-up time. And that was that. Back to the city we went.

My daughter Jeanette later told me they had a fantastic time spelunking. The cave they wanted to explore was entered by a hole in the ground. They used their ropes to descend. Jeanette confided in me that she was terrified that if an earthquake were to happen then, they would probably get sealed off and stuck in there. But all was well, and the exploring was a success.

While these eager explorers were continuing their adventure, my comadre Marilu and I were back at her house with our younger children: her daughter Carolina, her son Luis Eduardo, and my daughters María and Ana. We all would get together often, so the kids didn't mind staying back and playing together. They ran through the mango trees, swam for a while in my compadres' pool, and enjoyed our picnic. Soon it was time for Marilu and me to go retrieve the teenagers. The younger children remained at the house, as we needed all the space for the adventurers. We got our keys and were off.

Back we went, playing "Following the Leader" up that sinuous road. The kids were there waiting for us, so excited they could hardly contain themselves. The two vans filled up, and it was time to go back down the mountain.

If I didn't like going UP the mountain, I really didn't like going DOWN the mountain. Going down the curvy road was very frightening for me. I was afraid my brakes would go out, or I would lose control.

"Yikes. What's happening? Marilu, what are you doing?" CRASH. The bang was deafening. My eyes were wide open as I watched my wonderful friend switch lanes and drive right into the side of the mountain.

"What just happened?" We couldn't believe our eyes. The guys and girls started pouring out of her van, some all bloody, others unscathed but in a state of shock. And there was our beautiful Marilu, hunched over the steering wheel, no longer breathing. Her son Jose Alberto had been in the front passenger seat. He was distraught. He grabbed his mom in his arms. I went to comfort him. The kids dashed over to help the injured and try to figure out what to do next.

It all seems a blur now. Someone called the emergency number. I think it was Jose Alberto who called his father, my compadre[2] Pepe. Then we tried to take care of the wounded as best we could. I took the injured slowly and carefully the rest of the way down the mountain and back to the city to get help for them. The rest had to wait there until help arrived. Really, my memory fails me, and my daughter says the same thing. The next thing I remember is being back at my compadre Pepe's house with the friends that hadn't been hurt, and their parents all consoling my compadre and his son. My dear friend had already been taken away.

We don't understand why bad things happen to good people. My beloved comadre Marilu was a wonderful person—always willing to help anybody, and always active with the youth. We all loved her. It was devastating what happened to her. However, I know that in her last moments she was thinking of the children when she steered the car right into the rocks of that mountain. God guided her, and only she died. Many more people could have died that day. Her funeral was filled with youth and adults, all paying their respects. And I think everyone was having "God moments," realizing life is precious, life is frail, and we need to connect with God, our Savior.

And yes, good-bye, my dear friend. Until we meet again.

1. Comadre: special female friend who becomes a Godmother to the other person's child.
2. Compadre: special male friend who becomes a Godfather to the other person's child.

CHAPTER EIGHTEEN

The Pope Is Coming!

Out of the whole world, why would the pope decide to come to Tuxtla Gutierrez, Chiapas? We are on the southern border of Mexico with only the Usumacinta River between Guatemala and this state. And we're so isolated from the rest of the country. Everybody wondered about that, but, at the same time, everyone was elated. "Just think. The Pope is coming here!" could be heard everywhere.

Yes, there was so much enthusiasm. The proposed visit was creating a revival of sorts for the Catholics of the region—and even the non-Catholics. Everybody planned to witness such a big event. I was given the honor to be one of two people in Tuxtla to be assigned by the University to accompany the Pope's personal reporters to translate anything they needed and to answer any questions they might have. Well, they really didn't need translators. They knew so many languages. However, we did tell them about the region and the people, and whatever else they were curious about. We were taken to meet them at the Tuxtla airport and were fortunate enough to be right there as Pope John Paul disembarked from the plane. A Polish woman and her young son who lived in Tuxtla at that time met the pope at the bottom of the steps, and the boy, dressed all out in a Polish outfit, bowed before him and gave him a bouquet of flowers and a big welcome to Tuxtla in Polish. That definitely pleased the pope, as he was from Poland. Then, my Mexican counterpart and I were whisked off, along with the pope's reporters, to the field where the pope was to give his message to the people, while the pope was driven to the city's entrance so he could get into his popemobile and ride through the city and all the way out to the field where thousands of people were waiting for him. However, even out of all the hoopla, the joy, there also was tragedy…

"How could something like that happen? That's almost unbelievable." Besides the joy everyone was feeling, there was also much sorrow. The day before the pope's arrival, an airplane carrying thirty-eight passengers, all hoping to see the pope, was flying from the border city of Tapachula, Chiapas, and crashed en route near Arriaga. Twenty-seven people died.

Then, on Friday, May 10, 1990, cheers were heard from all over. People were standing on their roofs, on their balconies, lined up ten deep on the streets. They had gone to see their pope, the People's Pope. Such excitement. Such delight that the pope had chosen to visit them. And there he was, like a white angel, standing straight, waving at everybody, a big smile on his face. Flowers were landing on his popemobile. What enthusiasm. My daughters and my husband were watching it all from the huge windows of the Gran Hotel Humberto's restaurant. They were reveling in the moment, too.

Then the popemobile stopped. Pope John Paul II

Jan de la Fuente and me in the pressroom

descended from it and slowly entered the cathedral. All the coffins of the deceased were lined up inside waiting for the blessings of this beloved pope. Dignitaries were there to accompany the pope as he walked along and gave a special blessing over each of the coffins. What a sight it must have been.

And then the beloved pope was back in his popemobile and off to the designated place for his open-air mass. Pope John Paul II's personal press and my counterpart and I were already there when he arrived. The cheering for this man was deafening. The sight of those thousands of people—hundreds of thousands—like a field of bright yellow, giant sunflowers with huge smiles on their faces—the yellow symbolizing their support for their pope—was exhilarating. Some very talented local folks started playing their marimbas. People dressed in the apparel of various indigenous groups started approaching the altar and leaving the pope gifts. And then it was time for the holy man to speak.

I hardly remember what the pope had to say, I was so caught up in the moment. He prayed for a bishop and the other people who had died in that fateful plane crash. He spoke to all the people there. He told them to hold strong to their faith, to avoid the temptations of this world, and to refuse to aid the narcotics traffickers. He also had a message for the many refugees also attending to not give up hope, but to look to God. He said it pained him to see the suffering of the refugees and the sacrifices they were making to escape to a strange land with the hope of attaining better lives. He said they must keep God in their lives.

That same message resonates in this world today. More than thirty years later we have the same problems. The audience that day took it all in, and the enthusiasm for the pope, his presence, and his message continued to inspire all the people present there for a long time. I can attest to that.

CHAPTER NINETEEN

The Rise and Fall of My Earthly Rock

Yes, of course, my earthly rock at that time was my husband. Unlike our Heavenly Rock, who is steadfast and incapable of experiencing a downfall, we are all humans. When Fernando and I got married, my husband was mostly a pillar of his community. He was a hard worker respected for his intellect, admired for his sense of humor, and valued for his honesty. In many ways our relationship was wonderful. I was impressed by his intelligence. I loved his sense of humor. I was also swept away by his romanticism. Listening to him play intricate songs on the guitar, and sing and play the famous Mexican songs of the time with such gusto fascinated me. He was fiercely patriotic to his beloved Mexico, and his love for his country emanated from his every move. I was the same for my own country. We understood each other, and we loved to have a good time. This positive symbiotic relationship lasted for many years, although with some macho Mexicano moments mixed in.

When we got married, my father-in-law wasn't really convinced I was the girl for his oldest son. After all, American girls had quite a reputation in Mexico of being floozies—especially because of the way they were portrayed in American movies and in the news. It was the period of the '60s and '70s, the hippies, Woodstock, the antiwar movement, cultural change. I liked dressing in those bell bottom pants and short skirts, delighted in dancing disco, enjoyed taking my classes at Whitewater State, protesting the war (not the soldiers), and loved my God. That last characteristic governed the rest. My love for my God guided me in all my endeavors and made me who I was.

As I mentioned earlier, Fernando was an architect—and a very good one. He had finished all the required coursework, but he had never taken that last step to actually write and defend his thesis and take his final tests to get his diploma. He always said that was just a piece of paper. However, his outlook changed when I became pregnant, and he realized he was going to be a father. He wanted to make his profession official. While we were living in the house in El Desierto de los Leones, he went back to the Universidad Nacional Autónoma de Mexico and did that *encierro*, or confinement, with the other students wanting to get their diplomas. He spent many hours writing his thesis, studying with the other students of that generation, and studying on his own so that he could defend his thesis, pass the required tests, and get that coveted diploma. Of course, he was successful. And that is when I passed the test with my father-in-law. That's when he realized I was good for his precious son. And that "piece of paper" definitely influenced the quality of jobs Fernando was to get in the future.

Fernando was a proud, loving father. We all loved his cooking. He could whip up some scrumptious meals with whatever we had on hand. For me, his specialty was shrimp—any way he made it. He had the girls follow his directions to do all the prep, he cooked, we ate, and they cleaned up. It was terrific.

We loved traveling together with our friends Marilu and Pepe and their kids Jose Alberto, Carolina, and Luis Eduardo and, at other times, with our friends Paco, Mimi, and their daughter, Mimí Chica (little Mimí). With Marilu and Pepe, we went in our respective *combis* (Volkswagen minivans) that we had converted into campers to Cancún,

Tulúm, Xel-Há, Kohunlich, and Chichen Itzá of the Ruta Maya. We also took multiple trips to the Chiapas highlands of San Cristobal and nearby towns, and to the ocean beaches by Puerto Arista and Boca del Cielo (Mouth of Heaven) on the west coast of Chiapas. We took shorter trips with Paco, Mimi, and Mimi Chica, and thoroughly enjoyed those trips, also. We would go to the fields of the indigenous people in the highlands and pick vegetables and visit San Cristobol and other places.

We would also explore on our own. One time our small Volkswagen car had to be pulled out of a river by two oxen. I guess Fernando thought our car would just float across. Another time, as we were crossing a stream in our Volkswagen combi, Fernando stopped suddenly, and María went flying off her seat. She said she was ok, but days later, when we were playing a board game on the floor, she was favoring one arm over the other.

"María, does your arm hurt?" I asked. Why aren't you leaning on that one? We're going to have to take you to get X-rays to make sure you're okay."

Well, she wasn't okay. She had fractured her arm in that fall in the combi. The doctor fixed her up and put a cast on her arm, and off we went.

I think my husband's downfall really started when the peso devalued. He lost his focus. In 1970 the rate of the peso to the dollar was 12.50 to one. In 1980 the rate was about 23 to one. In 1985 the peso plunged even more. Our money was worth less and less. I had been sending the money I was making teaching up to my parents in Texas, and they'd deposit it in dollars in a joint account I had there with them. I used that money to pay for summer vacations to go up to El Paso with my daughters to visit them and to continue my education at the University of Texas at El Paso. Fernando thought I had a large amount stashed away up there, and he thought I was making way more in Tuxtla than he was at that time. Well, I certainly wasn't making the big bucks at the Universidad Autónoma de Chiapas, as they paid in pesos, and Mexican teachers, although venerated as scholars, didn't earn much money. I was making good money at the Instituto Bicultural, however, and I was paid in US dollars. Fernando had always refused to tell me how much he was making, so I didn't feel the need to tell him how much I was making, either. Maybe it would have been better if I had.

Another factor that may have contributed to his downfall was the fact that I had continued with my education and earned my bachelor's degree and my master's degree. That possibly influenced how he felt about me. He was always bragging me up with his friends, but when we were alone, he treated me differently. I sometimes told him that he should have married an easily intimidated Mexican woman that wouldn't challenge him instead of me. Even though I was young when we married, that was during the feminist movement, and I believed staunchly in it. (Was our relationship doomed from the start, and we didn't realize it?) I was receiving all the Ms. magazines, cofounded by Gloria Steinem and others, from the start, and I agreed with their message.

A bigger cause of Fernando's downfall was that, during those more difficult, later years of our marriage, he chose the wrong friends. Instead of spending time with his successful, positive friends, he'd keep company with other, less motivated ones. They'd sit around, drink, and whine about the devaluation of the Mexican money, the conditions of the world and of Mexico. When his good, successful friends would try to pull him out of his funk, he'd get angry with them and run to his other friends, instead.

With all of these factors in play, our family dynamics was also changing. With time, it became evident that our situation could not continue as it was...

Where was God in all this? As when I used my free will and decided to leave my family to join Fernando in marriage, Fernando had his free will here to make his own decisions. He was making poor choices. And he would not listen to good advice when his dear friends tried to reason with him. Our family situation was becoming difficult, but God opened another door for my daughters and me. I gave my daughters María and Ana the opportunity to provide input for our future. We could stay in Tuxtla and continue to live there as we were, or we could do as my best American friend there, Jan, had done, and go to make a new life in the US. I told them I was fine either way. I had great American friends, and I had great Mexican friends in Tuxtla. I could continue there, or we could change our lives drastically and go north to the United States. I certainly didn't want to make that big decision by myself and have my daughters possibly hold it against me for the rest of our lives. Well, they chose to move. My daughter Jeanette had already been living in El Paso, Texas, with Grandma Jan and Grandpa Bob, as she had gone there to continue her studies in the US after finishing the equivalent of high school in Tuxtla. Then, she found her special someone and got married there. I told María and Ana that we could join all our family there. And that's what we did.

I was blessed to have a good American friend who worked with the American-financed screwworm program in Tuxtla who was being transferred back to the United States. He told me that, as he was single and didn't have a lot of things to pack, there would be a lot of extra room in the moving truck, and I could ship my things to McAllen with his stuff for free, and then he would ship them to me in El Paso, and that's exactly what we did.

It seemed like everything was going full circle. Just as my mom had packed up those nine gigantic boxes for me when I got married and sent them to Eagle Pass so I could pick them up and take them to Mexico City when I was on my honeymoon, I packed up a multitude of boxes, stored them in my living room, and had them sent to McAllen, Texas, and from there to El Paso, Texas, so my daughters and I could have our things there. I know my husband didn't think we would go through with our plans, or maybe he thought we'd soon be back with him. He never said anything about all those boxes that were piling up in that front room. But, once we left, we made our home in El Paso. We flew there and were met by my parents. When Mom saw our dog carrier with us, she was curious and looked inside. Was she surprised to see FIVE little chihuahuas. And, just as Fernando and I had stayed for a couple of months with my in-laws after we got married, so María, Ana, those dogs, and I stayed with my parents for a couple of months while I got a job and found an apartment for us in El Paso.

Fernando had been my earthly rock for many years until life became too complicated, and it was time to move on. And my daughters and I were blessed to have a much stronger rock, an anchor, in our Heavenly Lord. And that has made all the difference.

And then it was time to open another door to another life—our life in the United States.

PART THREE

My Third Life

BACK TO THE UNITED STATES
(EL PASO): 1992 UNTIL NOW

CHAPTER TWENTY

Transition to a New Country and a New Life

Yes, a new door had been opened. María, Ana, and I had made our decisions to start a new life in the United States. Everything worked out, and there we were. I was back in the country I was born in, but in El Paso, close to my parents. My sister had gotten married since I had moved to Mexico, and she and her family were living in El Paso. My daughter Jeanette had found her special someone and had made her home there, also. We knew we would miss our Mexico, but we were optimistic about our future.

What was it like to move from one country to another like that? I was back in the US, but this time as a single mom. This was the first time I was really on my own since I got married twenty-two years earlier. I had no husband to rely on, to get help from. Luckily, I had my wonderful parents I knew I could count on if I really needed help. And they were the best role models a person could wish for to help me guide my daughters in the right direction. I had gotten my strong faith from them, and my daughters had gotten their strong faith from their and my examples.

I found a job teaching ESOL right away at Burges High School. That was a step in the right direction. Now that we knew where I was going to work and my daughters were going to go to school, the next step was to find a place to live, as we couldn't live with my parents forever.

"How about these apartments, girls? They are right behind the school. They have two pools, playground areas, a workout room, lots of walkways… The mall is right behind them." (I figured that would be a good selling point.)

María and Ana agreed those apartments seemed like the perfect place. And they were. My daughters made some good friends there that helped them make the transition to school in the US easier. I will write more about that transition later. Meanwhile, we had nothing to furnish our apartment with. We needed everything—right down to the silverware. I loved that my mom was enjoying helping me look for good bargains.

"Mom, I think I found a used wooden dining room set with eight chairs and a China cabinet that would be great for our apartment. Would you like to go with me to check it out?"

"Mom, there's a used living room set of a sofa, an armchair, an ottoman, and two end tables for sale. Will you come with me to look at it?"

"Mom, are you sure you want to go with me all the way to the Northeast to check out a bookcase? It's raining pretty hard." She did. I bought it. And I still have it. It brings back so many awesome memories of great times we spent together.

Mom and I drove all around El Paso looking for those and other good deals on items that my daughters and I needed for our small, two-bedroom apartment. All in all, it cost about $11,000 to furnish that place. And that was in 1992. Those were fun times I enjoyed with my mom. I was so blessed to have her in my life.

We lived in those apartments for two years. Then, I found what turned out to be the perfect house for us. It was also very close to our schools—about one and a half miles from Burges—just close enough, but not too close. It was so weird. The division between our school district and the adjoining one was right in the middle of our street.

The children that lived across the street from us went to Eastwood High School. My daughters went to MacArthur Middle School and Burges High School. The other side of the street was also on a different electrical grid, as they would still have electricity when ours went out and vice versa.

Well, we were going to be living on a teacher's salary—and a Texas teacher's salary, at that. Luckily, the school district gave me credit for eight years of teaching for the years I taught in Tuxtla, although I had actually taught many more years than that when you count the years at the Instituto Bicultural and also the years at the UACH. Mom told me to be happy they gave me the eight years, and I guess I was, as those eight years put me higher on the salary schedule than a beginning teacher's salary. However, I had been making more at the Instituto Bicultural in Tuxtla in Mexico when I left there than what I started out earning at Burges.

To make ends meet, I took on as many other "jobs" as I could. (I really enjoyed them, so I hardly considered them "work.") At one time I was working four jobs simultaneously: as a teacher, a teacher union building rep, an American Federation of Teachers Union Teacher Trainer giving classes on the weekends and some evenings to teachers for their continuing education credits, and curriculum writing, mainly during the summers, for the ESOL courses of the district. All of that certainly kept me busy, especially while I was trying to bring up my two daughters at the same time.

How did I manage? Financially, we had to keep a strict budget. My suggestion: go to stores as infrequently as possible to limit spontaneous purchases. (I still do.)

And how did I manage raising my daughters? Being a teacher had its advantages. I had the same holidays and vacation days as my daughters. Also, teaching students relatively the same ages as my daughters,

I could relate to what my students were going through and what my daughters were going through. However, living as a single mom with two children at home could be quite a challenge. In fact, at times it seemed overwhelming. When I felt that way, my solution was to go to God and ask Him for His peace and His help. With two young daughters—Ana in sixth grade and María in eleventh grade, sometimes there were some quite ugly interactions between them. I found solace in my faith. At those times, I would lie in bed and cry myself to sleep when they were fighting and yelling at each other, or I would read my little devotional booklets, calm down, and ask God for guidance.

I made every effort to promote family harmony and create fun memories for us through a variety of family activities: board games, movie nights, travel, walking dogs, (we had the five chihuahuas we had brought up to the States until we moved into our own home) and, of course, doing things with the grandparents. Every Tuesday night my daughters and I would meet Jeanette and my grandson Michael (yes, I had become a grandmother), my sister and her family, and my parents for Tuesday night dinners together at the food court at Basset Center. Those get-togethers were great because we could all meet and get what we wanted to eat, but nobody had to cook, and nobody had to clean up.

The transition to life in the US was hardest on María. She had been the daughter closest to her dad, and she had had so many good friends in Tuxtla. Ana was still in grade school, and by the time I had her, we didn't have as many friends with children her age she could hang out with, so she didn't have the ties to Tuxtla that her sister did.

None of my daughters had any trouble academically when we came up. Jeanette had come up earlier and stayed with my parents while she studied interior design after she finished the equivalent of high school in Mexico. She graduated with straight As in all her courses. María said she was way ahead of the American students in her math classes. She never liked to read, so, for her English classes, she never read a book. She'd always ask her friends what the stories they were studying were about and wing it. And I was an ESOL teacher at her school. And I loved English reading and writing. To each his or her own. She always did well in all her classes, too, though. Ana started in sixth grade when we came up to the States, but she had no problem, as she studied her last year in Tuxtla in the Instituto Bicultural, where I was teaching, and all the classes except Spanish were taught in English. I was even her English teacher that year.

While Jeanette was living with Grandma Jan and Grandpa Bob and taking her interior design courses, she started working at Skaggs Alpha Beta—now known as Albertson's. She started out bagging groceries because she wasn't eighteen yet. As soon as she turned eighteen, she started working in the video department/lobby as a clerk cashing checks, preparing money orders, renting out movies and everything else she needed to do there. Then, she became the lobby supervisor. Soon after that, they promoted her to nonfood supervisor. And, at twenty-four years old, she became the manager of the whole store. She had more than one hundred employees under her control. She was moved to two other stores, but always as the store manager. Jeanette continued working for Albertson's until just a few months short of thirty years of service. Now, she and her husband are owners of a property restoration company in El Paso.

After María graduated from Burges, she started working for a telephone company. She had to drive to get to the offices. At first, they were close to my school. Later, the company moved downtown. As I was at Burges all day, and we only had one car, I had her take Ana and me to MacArthur and Burges. Then she could have my car until she was done with her work, at which time she'd go back and pick us up. It all worked out ok. She has continued working at that telephone company. She definitely took advantage of her Spanish for her calls there and earned a stipend for that ability.

After Ana graduated from St. Edwards University, she started working for a beer company. She continued working there until she switched to a liquor company. She enjoys working there now. Those companies have been good to her, and she has had much to offer them. She's the only one of my immediate family who doesn't live in El Paso. She lives in Phoenix, Arizona.

That's quite a lot to digest here: our arrival to a new country for my daughters, my finding a job and a place to live, and our adapting to our new lives. The new door had opened, and we embraced our new lives with enthusiasm. God was with us every step of the way.

CHAPTER TWENTY-ONE

You Can Have the Boys!

Yes, I always wanted three daughters, and God answered my prayers. My parents had had three children: my brother, my sister, and me. I thought that would be the perfect number for me, although I wanted three daughters. And that's just what God gave me. And I would jokingly tell my daughters that they could have the boys. Well, that's how it worked out for my first three grandchildren. Jeanette had my first grandson, Michael. María had the next two grandsons, Luis and Cristopher.

Michael was the apple of my parents' eyes. He was their very first grandchild, and he was a sweetheart. He is a very sensitive person and cares deeply about all the people who surround him. A perfect example relating to his grandfather Bob is one time when his grandpa was in rehab at a facility in El Paso. Michael took his trombone, found out which room his grandpa was staying in, and stood outside by the room's window amd gave Grandpa Bob a recital just for him. Needless to say, Grandpa Bob never forgot that expression of love from his grandson. Another example, this time related to Grandma Jan after Grandpa Bob had died, was when Michael organized a private movie night for the two of them. Michael popped popcorn, got them drinks, moved the armchairs around to simulate a movie theater showroom, closed the curtains, and put on a movie he knew Grandma Jan would enjoy. That sure made her feel special. These are just a couple of examples of Michael's thoughtfulness.

Then it was María's turn to have children, and, yes, she had two boys, and both within fourteen months of each other. She sure had her hands full. She was still working at the telephone company, too. We were continuing our Tuesday night family get-togethers at the food court at Basset Center Mall, and in she would come with her double stroller with her two baby boys. Our group was getting bigger and bigger.

As those boys grew up, they gave María lots of satisfaction and love, but they were also very playful, bordering on mischievous. Here's one example: Maria had taken the seeds out of some of the pomegranates from her tree and given some to her sons to eat. She went to take a nap, and the boys, about two and three years old at the time, got more pomegranate seeds and proceeded to gleefully throw them up in the air and let them fall on her carpet in the TV room. As Maria was resting, she heard her sons having fun and thought, "How sweet!"

However, when she got up, what she saw almost gave her a heart attack. Pomegranate seeds are almost impossible to get out of clothing or carpets. Luckily, her carpet was a dark brown and didn't show the red stains too much. (That convinced me I was right desiring to have three girls.) And that wasn't the last time for such impish activity. Another time María took a nap, her little boys found a bag of potato chips. Well, they had a grand old time taking the chips out of the bag, throwing them around the room, and then running around stomping on them. There ensued another great opportunity for a heart attack when María realized what was happening. (That my desire to have three girls was a good idea was confirmed once again.) María then realized it could be risky to take a nap when her sons were awake.

When Luis was in high school, he was active in Student Council, and he played in the band. He started out playing the flute that I had used when I played in the band in my high school. He soon switched over to the trumpet. A hilarious anecdote involving Luis is one time when

I accompanied María to watch Luis play in the Eastwood High School marching band for a battle of the high school bands at the Socorro Athletic Complex, or SAC, a multipurpose stadium. We waited patiently for the Eastwood band's time to play. We really enjoyed watching all the bands play and march. They all looked so professional—just like the college bands marching at their teams' half-times. When it was almost time for his band, I got my video recorder ready. We watched the performance enthusiastically. I tried my best to film Luis marching. He was six feet five inches tall, so I thought it wouldn't be that hard to film him—just look for a very tall trumpet player. Well, when it was all over, and we were watching it together later, Luis exclaimed, "Grandma, that's not me. You filmed a different tall trumpet player!" I sure felt embarrassed—and sad that I hadn't gotten Luis on tape.

Luis also loves to bake, and he baked some delicious treats for Grandma Jan. (Grandpa Bob had died years earlier.) Grandma Jan's favorites were his lemon bars and some absolutely delicious peaches-n-cream cheesecakes that were pleasing to the eyes with their peach slices delicately positioned in the transparent gelatin on top of the cheesecakes. Grandma Jan was so excited to get them and be able to slice them up and proudly distribute the slices to her friends at the independent living place where she had her apartment.

Cris played football on a city team when he was little, and María and I enjoyed going to the parks to cheer him on. Cris got tackled quite hard many times, which concerned us. He continued playing football, though, and also played basketball and soccer. He loved wrestling, too, but one time he was jostled quite hard, resulting in a concussion. That definitely worried us. He was great at all the sports.

Well, those were the boys. Then it was time to have the girls. Ana had my first granddaughter, Lilyana. There was a fourteen-year gap between my youngest grandson, Cris, and Lily. She was—and is—a very sweet young girl. She has taken gymnastics and swimming classes. She loves to volunteer to help others at a variety of functions. María and I went with Lily and her mom to a Feed My Starving Children once (Ana and Lily serve there often). Lily got especially excited about being accepted to be a student leader for younger children at the summer camp at her church. That was a big honor. Speaking of honors, Lily is always listed on her school's honor roll.

And then there is Sophia, my youngest grandchild, and another honor roll student. Jeanette has my oldest grandchild, Michael, and my youngest grandchild, Sophia. They are twenty-one years and three months apart in age. Sophia is two years younger than Lily. She is only nine years old, but already she has distinguished herself as a fantastic dancer, winning countless awards and dance scholarships. She is constantly standing with one leg straight up in the air or moving around in other unnatural positions wherever she is. My friend Yvette calls her a pretzel. Sophia sure has amazing balance, and she keeps Jeanette and Carlo busy taking her to dance competitions in-state and out-of-state. She has also participated in the Joffrey Ballet training program in Miami, Florida, after receiving a scholarship for that at one of her dance competitions.

I guess her performance prowess began at an even younger age, though…

"Look at her sing. Look at her moving, feeling the music. All the other children are just standing there, barely mouthing the words. Sophia is really enjoying herself."

That was referring to Sophia at one month shy of two years old performing on stage at her daycare center Flying Colors. Her "show" was so memorable that I can still see her singing and dancing to the music to this day.

And those are my grandchildren. God gave me my girls, and they had the boys—as well as a couple of girls. God has blessed us all immensely.

I wanted to include this chapter in my life, as I wanted these stories to live on for my family and for posterity. Also, I wanted to give hope to parents living God-fearing, God-loving lives who are good examples for their children that their examples will, God willing, result in the next generation following in their footsteps. My grandchildren seem to be on the right paths, and I thank the Lord.

CHAPTER TWENTY-TWO

Chamo

And then there was Chamo, the best "gift" I was ever given—the cutest, sweetest, little Bichon Frisé, and my loyal companion for eighteen years. He kept me fit, as we would take long walks together three times a day through rain, shine, and even the few snow days we would have in El Paso. He was the reason I got to know my neighbors near and far, as we'd stop, and I'd chat with the people along the way. He was the object of much affection from my family, my friends, and me.

Join me in enjoying his existence…

There he goes, racing excitedly around and around in circles in the backyard and in the house doing the "Bichon Blitz," often with my grandson Cris chasing him with delight. Here we come, my granddaughter Sophia pushing her baby doll in her stroller, while Chamo and I accompany them on their "journey." Neighbors could see many combinations of my grandchildren, Chamo, and me walking around the block and enjoying each other's company. And later, Chamo and I were blessed with daily walks with my daughter María and her two adorable, but very noisy schnauzers, as we meandered through our neighborhoods getting our much-needed exercise and enjoying the fresh air. As Chamo got older, it became more and more difficult for him to walk, so we needed to make modifications. Soon we were zooming around, Chamo in his doggie stroller, his head held high, his ears blowing in the wind, and a big smile on his face.

We grew "old" together. And when it became necessary to say goodbye and send him off to doggie heaven, I was blessed to have my daughter Ana and my granddaughter Lily by my side. The same daughter who had given Chamo to me eighteen years earlier was there at his demise. And she and Lily, who loved Chamo dearly, too, had just gone through the same difficult situation with two of their own beloved dogs. They understood what I was going through and were there to console me.

How did Chamo become mine? Well, my daughter Ana was living in Denver, Colorado, and had to go on a business trip. She had just bought Chamo and finished house training him. She didn't have anyone to leave him with, and she certainly didn't want to leave him in a boarding facility. Who could she turn to? Her mother, of course. Ana drove Chamo to El Paso and left him with me, saying she'd be back to pick him up as soon as possible—no later than a month. Well, one month turned into two, then

three... Then she was ready to pick up her little one. However, I was not ready to give him up. I gave her the news that after three months, Chamo was mine. Ana could come and visit him.

And his name? Chamo means *friend* in a language spoken in Peru. Ana had traveled to Peru just before purchasing him, and she thought that name would be very apropos—and it certainly was.

CHAPTER TWENTY-THREE
Near Death!

There she is, one of many in a sea of dark purple gowns. All the graduates, including my youngest daughter, Ana, were marching ceremoniously into the Don Haskin's Center of the University of Texas-El Paso to find their seats for the big moment, their graduation from Burges High School. Our whole family was there for the big day. All the students were so excited. Soon they would be out in the real world. And then, days later . . .

"Mom, I lost control," my daughter Ana shrieked. "We're going down!"

I had no idea what was happening. My daughter was driving our car. We were on our way to celebrate her high school graduation with a special trip to Colorado—specifically to Durango and Pagosa Springs. We had so been looking forward to it. Then she'd be off to St. Edwards University in Austin, Texas, to continue her education. This was our first day of the trip. I was in the passenger seat reading newspapers I had brought along, confident that everything would go just as planned. However, it didn't.

Bang, boom, crash. The car hit loose gravel on the I-25. The car swerved. Ana overcorrected. And there we were zooming down the embankment. And then it happened: the ear-piercing sound of grating, scraping, grinding, and banging of the car against the rocky ground. The car rolled over FIVE times—not sideways, but top to bottom front over back. I can still hear those grinding, scratching sounds in my head as if it were happening right now, twenty-four years later.

Finally, it stopped. Ana was sitting in the passenger seat in pain. I was totally turned around in my seat looking at the back seat. How did that happen? There was blood all over the left side of the back seat. Somehow, in all that flipping over and over, my elbow must have unfastened the seat belt, which was all pulled out and hanging loose. I must have been flying around. In all that commotion, my head hit the visor and bent it in half, and the window ended up open and smashed a bit. My left elbow had hit it hard and got a deep gash, the source of the blood. The gash was also full of tiny stones and dirt. Imagine how that happened. I think I was semiconscious. We were both stunned.

And in that instant, our guardian angels appeared. There's no other way to interpret this. A car had been behind us. There had been very little traffic on that road until then. The couple in the car had seen the whole accident. I thank the Lord that they stopped to render aid, as they had a small child and could have just continued on their way, not wanting the child to experience what ensued. And the husband was a paramedic, and the wife was a nurse. What are the odds? And they had a cell phone. This happened on July 26, 1999. Not that many people had cell phones at that time. Even with this terrible accident, God was with us. I have no doubt.

The two adults bolted from their car and ran to reach us. The woman checked out Ana, while the husband was assessing my situation. He very carefully turned me around in my seat and was trying to determine the damage. While they were attending to us, they also called 911 to request help. These angels stayed with us until the ambulance arrived and the police arrived, to whom they gave an eye-witness report.

I was barely aware of what was happening. All I remember is being pulled out of the car and being put on a very hard board, being strapped in, and being put in the ambulance. My thoughts were, "Where was my daughter? How was she?" When I realized that she was in the emergency vehicle with me, I told her, "Don't worry, Ana. We'll get cleaned up and continue our vacation." Obviously, I didn't realize the extent of my injuries.

We were then transported to Socorro General Hospital in Socorro, New Mexico, a super- small town on the way to Albuquerque, New Mexico, which was to be the first stop of our journey, where we had planned on visiting my Uncle Bruce and my Aunt Shirley. Well, we didn't make it there, but Ana gave the authorities Uncle Bruce's contact information, and when he found out about our accident, he drove to Socorro to be with us and help us however he could. (He was closer to us than our family members in El Paso were.) Just seeing his big smile and hearing his voice was heaven to my eyes and ears. And my daughter was there with me, so frightened, so worried. Seeing her so distraught broke my heart.

Thank goodness we had been traveling in our 1993 Buick, a very sturdy car. One of the tires had flown off. The car was totaled. It was all crashed in. And yet, WE WERE ALIVE. Ana's fingers were black and blue from holding on to the steering wheel so hard, trying to get control of the car. Her body was aching from hitting the steering wheel so hard. I don't remember an air bag inflating. Maybe the car didn't have one. Other than that, and being in a state of shock, Ana was okay.

It was a different story for me. I ended up with a fractured pelvis, a broken left knee, a broken right ankle, a deep gash by my left elbow, and four broken ribs, as well as a lot of bruises. (A doctor told me later that if I had had any more pressure put on those ribs, I would have died. That's what would have killed me.) The doctors at the hospital in Socorro cleaned the deep wound of my left elbow and proceeded to give me seven stitches to sew it up, then they took X-rays of everything. The X-rays didn't show the extent of the injuries because everything was so inflamed. They did what they could, knowing I needed to get back home to continue whatever treatment was needed. When the doctors finally cleared me to travel back to El Paso, they told me I should follow up for treatment of all my injuries there as soon as possible, and it was time to go home. Our exciting vacation had taken quite a turn.

Jim, a very special friend of mine, drove up from El Paso to take us back. On the way up, he had stopped to check out the car where it was being held. After seeing it, he couldn't believe we were still alive—and that Ana was hardly hurt.

"You guys sure were lucky," he said.

"It wasn't luck," I said, "It was God by our side."

Then the next phase of this adventure began. Back in El Paso, I went to see my doctor. During that first visit, he looked at the X-rays they had taken in Socorro, didn't take any new ones, looked at the stitches in my arm, and told me I could walk without crutches; I just needed to wear a gigantic boot he ordered for my right ankle. As I mentioned before, the X-rays after the accident didn't show the full extent of the injuries, but any conscientious doctor should have delved a lot further into what was wrong. I trusted him and left thinking I just needed to try to stay off my feet. He let me go with strong painkillers and a broken knee and a broken ankle to walk on.

One week later, this same doctor (whom I won't name, as I don't want to put myself in jeopardy, but I firmly believe should have been accused of malpractice), took the stitches out of my elbow and gave me one referral for physical therapy and one for a doctor to evaluate my ankle. And that was that.

On Friday, August 14th, nineteen days after the accident, I had my appointment with Dr. King, a Godsend. He actually saved my legs from a lot of future suffering. After reviewing my situation and taking new X-rays, he announced he couldn't believe I was walking like that—that my left knee was broken, and my right ankle was also broken. He was livid. He was incredulous that another doctor could have been so inept.

"There is a golden period in which breaks like these have to be taken care of for them to heal correctly," he explained. "You are at the very end of this golden period. I am fully booked on Monday, but I want you in early, and you will be my first patient for surgery."

That was on a Friday. And first thing Monday, August 18th, there I was in Sierra Medical Hospital waiting for just that—and I was very scared. I kept telling everybody, "Left knee and right ankle" over and over again. I had heard so many horror stories of surgeries being done on wrong limbs, things being left in bodies when they are sewn up… Then somebody wrote on my left knee and my right ankle, and I felt relieved. After that I calmed down a bit.

And just like that the surgery was all over. I was in a room to recuperate. I was having the hardest time coming out of the anesthesia. I remember I could see all the little lines on the ceiling, but I couldn't come to. Finally, I did, and there was my mother by my side. Bless the Lord. And God bless my mom.

I followed Dr. King's instructions to the letter. I now have a six and three-quarter inch, very straight scar on my left knee and a scar in a circle around three quarters of my right ankle. And I never feel pain when it's cold or at any other time from those breaks. I am so grateful to this wonderful doctor.

My ordeal was not over. Next came the recuperation. I needed to get around in a wheelchair while I was healing. Well, the hallways at my house were so narrow that the wheelchair couldn't maneuver around them, so I had to stay at my parents' house. I was so blessed to have healthy parents willing to take care of me. I was able to stay in my brother's former bedroom and work my knee in the bedroom that faced the street. I was lucky they had that room, as the machine I needed to use to get my knee functioning correctly was very big and heavy. We just left it there on the bed so that I could use it as need be.

Mom or Dad had to set the correct angle for the machine to move my leg, and I'd have to just lie there and let the machine move my leg for me for the designated amount of time.

"Hang in there. You're going through a lot now, but in the future, everything will just be a memory." My mom would say that to me often. And I have given that same advice later to many people I know that were going through difficulties of their own.

Sometime later:

"My head is throbbing. It's really hurting. The pain is unreal!" The saga continued. My parents and I were on our way to meet my other two daughters, Jeanette and María, at a restaurant when my head felt like it was going to explode. My father beelined it for the nearest hospital, and I was admitted, and on September 30th, over two months after the car accident, I was having craniotomy surgery by Dr. Chang for acute bilateral frontal subdural hematomas. Imagine that. He had to relieve the pressure on the brain, so he drilled two holes on the top of my head, one on each side, and connected tubes for drainage. I guess that felt better. And I was in the hospital again. I wonder if my head hitting my car's visor so hard during the accident had anything to do with this new situation.

My parents and daughters would come and visit, but they wouldn't lend me a mirror to let me see what I looked like with those tubes coming out of my head. They thought I'd freak out. And then, one day my niece Jennifer visited. I asked her for a mirror.

"Ya, sure," she said. "Here."

Well, I didn't freak out. I just thought I looked like a Martian or something with those tubes protruding from my head and ending in some small, round containers. We had a good laugh when I told her that was the first time I had seen them and why.

Finally, I was better and able to stay in my own house. I was on disability from my job at Burges High School for almost a full semester.

When I did go back in November, I only had one half-day of sick leave left for the whole rest of the year. It's a good thing I had been pretty healthy before all this and had built up almost a semester of sick days I could use.

As for my youngest daughter, Ana, my companion on this memorable trip, she had wanted to stay in El Paso to take care of me instead of going away to college. I couldn't let her do that. I told her she needed to go to her new destination, St. Edwards University, and make me proud. Her two older sisters and her grandparents would take care of me. And so it was. Four years later she was honored with the President's Award and graduated summa cum laude from that same St. Edward's University.

I have no doubt that God was with us throughout this challenging time. I learned that life can change in a moment, and having the love and support of family during such a difficult time is a blessing that helps us get through it. I gained even more respect for the medical profession. Lastly, it's amazing how our bodies can heal with time. It's truly miraculous.

Be careful for nothing; but in every thing by prayer and supplication with thanksgiving let your requests be known unto God. And the peace of God, which passeth all understanding, shall keep your hearts and minds through Christ Jesus.   Philippians 4:6-7.

Yes, we will experience tough times, but we need to remember that God is guiding us and protecting us through our life journeys. No matter what happens to us, God is our refuge, our rock, our hope. And our family are the people who are there for us through thick and thin, love us unconditionally, and give us comfort and joy.

CHAPTER TWENTY-FOUR

Pickles or Mustard?

Professional development for teachers is often not our favorite place to be. However, when we have professional development for all the ESOL high school teachers of our district, or ESOL teachers by district areas, we really do enjoy these meetings. They are special days when we are able to gather, to share our expertise, to bond. Through the years we have forged very special friendships. Well, one of these meetings at the Professional Development Center did not go so well for me.

"AYYY!" I exclaimed as I was falling out of my chair almost to the floor with the most agonizing pain in my leg. It had happened again—that horrendous pain that is indescribable. And all I could do was just "sit" there, my body twisting into bizarre contortions as everybody looked on. Finally, after what seemed like an eternity, the pain subsided, and I was able to sit normally again in my chair. Unfortunately, such cramps were almost commonplace for me.

Another day, another place. There I was sitting on one of those uncomfortable, hard, plastic chairs in one of the meeting rooms at Burges High School. The meeting was in session, when, all of a sudden, I got another painful cramp in my calf. I screamed in pain and squirmed in my chair. No matter how I positioned myself, I felt an excruciating pain in my leg. This was in front of the whole English department. I couldn't even think about feeling embarrassed at that moment; the pain was too much. (I definitely did feel embarrassed about it all later, though.)

"Somebody go to the cafeteria and get some packages of mustard, quick," shouted out my colleague Laura. There were looks of apprehension, looks of bewilderment, looks of helplessness. It was obvious I was in great pain.

Well, someone did dash out to find some mustard packets. The meeting was at a standstill. I, unfortunately, was the center of attention.

Finally, my "savior" of the moment arrived. I gobbled down four to five packets of that bright, yellow, strong, condiment. In a matter of only a couple of minutes, I was fine. That marvelous mustard had done the trick.

Everyone was amazed. We were all looking at Laura and wondering how she knew what to do. She explained that in her interactions with coaches at Burges, she learned that was how leg cramps were taken care of on the field during practice and at games. I must say, I sure was ecstatic that she had known that. And all the participants of that fateful meeting were gifted with this new knowledge, also.

I can't tell you the number of times I have relied on this knowledge of the power of this tangy, hot, strong substance. I have mustard packets on my nightstand, in my car, in my purse, in my study, next to the TV—almost everywhere. As I told you earlier, I was once a Girl Scout, and I know how to be prepared. My painful experiences have also affected my family. In addition to feeling sorry for me when they watch me writhe in pain, they have become active participants, always making sure they have mustard on hand—and when they go to fast food places or movie theaters, they always pick up mustard packages for me. Everybody in my family knows about the effectiveness of this yellow miracle. I start getting a cramp, and someone always yells out, "Get the mustard!" Sometimes, however, certainly mocking my solution, my granddaughter Sophia will yell out, "Get the catsup. Get the catsup!" I'm not quite sure what to make of that.

Yes, I always try to be prepared. However, there I was once at the movie theater in Phoenix with my daughter Ana and my granddaughter Lilyana. We were watching the movie "Cars," when one of those dreaded cramps occurred. Oops. That time I wasn't prepared, and my daughter ended up having to leave the theater and go to a concession stand in the lobby to get some coveted packages of mustard. They did the trick, though. Other times, when I forget to stash my bedstand with those packets, and I get those loathsome cramps, or charlie horses, it can take me a very long time to get to the kitchen for my remedy. I can barely walk. I cannot even stand up straight. I can't recover until I have my mustard.

As for my title "Pickles or Mustard?", pickles or pickle juice will have the same effect on cramps. So, what's your choice, pickles or mustard?

CHAPTER TWENTY-FIVE

I Can See!

"Wow. Look at those amazing colors. The blues are so dazzling. The reds are so flaming. They all are so vivid. What have I been missing all these years?"

Yes, there I was in the recovery room, my mother sitting on a chair by my side. She looked at me quizzically, wondering what I was talking about. I was looking at the old, faded curtains separating my mom and me from fellow patients who had also had cataract surgery. However, I guess I hadn't seen colors like those in a long time. You see, I had cataracts in both eyes, and my eye doctor kept telling me I'd need surgery, but that my eyes weren't "ripe" yet.

"Ripe? What's that all about?" I thought. I had been seeing "halos" around traffic lights and streetlights for what seemed like ages. It was getting hard to see to drive at night. I certainly thought I was ready, but I was made to wait several more years before the windows to that bright, mesmerizing world were opened.

I had used glasses since first grade. You can pick me out in my first-grade class picture. I'm the little girl with the bowl haircut and the pointed, red and white striped glasses, which would have been the perfect accessory for the volunteer Candy Stripers of that time. Every year I would go for a new eye exam. And every year I would get new glasses.

"Wow. Look at the blades of grass. Look at the leaves on the trees." My reactions to my new glasses were always instantaneous—I could see sharply again. What a gift of newly acquired visual acuity.

That went on for eight years—all through grade school and junior high. In summer, my glasses would sometimes slide down my nose when I was sweating. In winter, my glasses would steam up every time I would walk from the bitter Wisconsin cold into a warm building. Then, I wouldn't be able to see. If you wear glasses, you know what I'm talking about.

Finally, during my freshman year of high school, I got contacts. The first time I tried them on, I couldn't get them out. The eye doctor had to take them out with a little suction cup wand. After at least a half hour of practicing taking them out and putting them back in, I was given the go-ahead, and my parents and I went back home.

I loved not having to wear glasses anymore. Contacts were the greatest. Without them, I was just one step away from needing a seeing-eye dog. However, as soon as I would pop them in, sight was restored. Using contacts did have its moments, though. There were instances when the contacts didn't want to behave. I remember one time when I was babysitting about a mile from home. The little boy I was taking care of pushed me while we were playing. Out flew one of my contacts. I couldn't find it anywhere—and I was afraid he would step on it. I called my home, and my loving, dependable brother swiftly ran right over and looked until he found it. I was blessed.

Once in a while a contact would fly out of my eye at a party, or in church, or just about anywhere. Then it was everybody to the rescue until it was found. I don't know if soft contacts behave the same way. I've always used hard, gas permeable ones. My eye doctors said that for my extremely bad eyesight, the hard ones would be the best. Those contacts would keep the shape of the eyes, and there wouldn't be such a huge contrast in my vision from one year to the next as I had when I used glasses. They were right. I kept pretty much the same correction until I developed the cataracts.

As I got older, I was developing cataracts. At first, I didn't realize that, but as the years went by, I was starting to see halos around the stop lights and streetlights. My eye doctor said for at least five years that my eyes weren't ready for surgery yet, though. My eyes weren't RIPE. What a concept. Ripe eyes. Well, I guess that's what all doctors refer to that condition as. And finally, they were ripe. First, I had one eye operated on. Two years later, the other eye was ripe—and ready for that surgery. Then I could see so well that I joked I had bionic eyes.

I thank my ophthalmologist for the gift of sight—glasses-and contacts-free. And I thank the Lord for guiding the surgeon's hands as he conducted the surgeries.

If you ever do get cataracts—and you probably will if you live long enough—don't be afraid to have cataract surgery. In the hands of a capable doctor, there's nothing to it. And you will enjoy those vibrant colors once again.

CHAPTER TWENTY-SIX

Don't Leave Your Keys in the Door!

Have you ever left your keys in the door? Have you ever brought groceries—or something else—into your house and gotten so busy you forgot to take your keys out of the door...and then later just closed the door? I know I have, and too many times that I'd care to admit, especially since my daughters are always reminding me not to leave my keys there. I know a lot of other people have done the same, but how about leaving your keys on the INSIDE of the door? That should be safe, right? Well, don't count on it.

That's where this story starts. It was an ordinary day—or so I thought. I got up, took care of business, made my bed, and went to the kitchen for my morning coffee.

"Hmm, that's weird. Why would that door be open a little?" It was strange. I always close everything up before I retire for the evening. However, upon closer inspection, I saw that there was a hole in the screen door, and that THAT door was open, too. (That door opens to the outside, so it wasn't immediately evident.)

What was going on? Walking into the sunroom, I smelled a strange, pungent odor. It was wine. And there it was—a broken wine bottle in the corner by the sliding glass door to the outside. What on earth happened here?

"Oh my God. Thank the Lord." This situation could have really taken a turn for the worse. When I finally came to my senses, I realized my house had been broken into—and with ME IN IT. There's nothing like being such a sound sleeper, and a little hard of hearing, and having a dog that is almost deaf except, of course, leaving the key in the door.

What to do next? Call my son-in-law, Carlo, of course. Then call the police. Well, Carlo was at my house in a flash for moral support and advice. Soon after, the police arrived. A couple of officers immediately got busy dusting everything for fingerprints, while one of them took down all of the necessary information. And just like that they were gone. Carlo stayed until I had calmed down, and then I was alone to process what had just happened.

Well, as I mentioned at the beginning, I had inadvertently left the keys in the wooden door used to enter my house from the back yard. I thought I had locked it, but I guess I had just closed it and left it like that. A bold young man had had the audacity to break into my house—TO BREAK INTO MY HOUSE. He had slid open the glass sliding door to the sunroom and noticed my long pruning shears I had placed next to the screen door, so I'd have them to prune more bushes when I felt like it. What a "present". Just the thing he needed to cut a hole in the metal screen. And "present number two," there were the keys in the keyhole of the wooden door to get in. This guy had hit the jackpot. So, he ventured in, looked around, and **took a wine bottle out of my fridge.**

I really don't know much more than that. I don't know what time this happened. As I mentioned before, my little dog and I were sound asleep and didn't hear a thing. **Something** made this person run out the back door, obviously in a panic. He dropped the wine bottle as he was fleeing. I don't know if he had taken the liberty of exploring the whole house, or what. I didn't notice anything else taken from inside the house, although I had noticed that a gas trimmer that I had put under a sofa in the sunroom was missing. I suspect the intruder walked into the house, toward my bedroom, noticed a person covered up in the bed, and ran out, panicky. He left the door open, and off he went. And that was that.

Less than a week later, I got a call from the police station. They had found the object the villain used to cut the screen door. It wasn't even the garden shears. It was the gas trimmer that I had left under the sofa in the sunroom. Its mint green color was the giveaway. The police knew that one was mine. The thief had tried to pawn it not far away. And that person lived less than a mile away from me. I don't know what the police threatened him with, but they told me I shouldn't have to worry about him anymore.

Yes, Oh, my God. Thank the Lord. This incident could have ended very differently.

Something terrifying could have happened to me. Something made this thief run off. I have no doubt this was one of my "God moments". God saved me. And I am so grateful.

And there will be no more keys left in the door!

And the Lord, He *is* the One who goes before you. He will be with you, He will not leave you nor forsake you; do not fear nor be dismayed.

Deuteronomy 31:8.

CHAPTER TWENTY-SEVEN

Thank You, God!

Sunday, April 16: Did You Hear That?

Sunday Funday. Yes, another wonderful day with family. Now that Jeanette has moved so far from us (at least for me. I really don't feel comfortable driving there myself anymore), I am blessed with a wonderful daughter who lives near me. She picks me up, and off we go.

So, this Sunday the weather was cooperating, and we made it a swim day. María, her two dogs, and I joined Jeanette, my granddaughter Sophia, and their two dogs at their house for lunch and a swim. The water was cold, but we really wanted to have fun in the sun—or water.

"Come on, Mom. It's not that cold. You can get in faster than that!"

It took me about forty minutes to finally get wet enough to be able to jump around in the water and do some exercises while we all chatted about a multitude of topics. Sophia had loads of fun doing fancy maneuvers and showing us her skills in the water and on the trampoline.

After that fun in the pool, we got everything ready for our lunch and ate it poolside, enjoying the view and watching all the dogs play together. Carlo, Jeanette's husband, got home from the trip he had taken and joined us for lunch. We are all so blessed that we get along so well.

Soon, it was time to go back home. I got busy getting all my things together. Once I was done, Jeanette unlocked the front door so I could get out to the car. It was then that I heard a dog bark.

"Wow, I hear a dog that barks just like Max," I exclaimed. Max, María's oldest dog, has a very distinct, high-pitched bark when he's excited. I thought it strange that another dog would be barking exactly like him.

My daughter María was outside cutting pieces off a big plant. When she heard me say that she looked around for her Max and darted down the very long driveway toward the  entrance to Jeanette's property. Behind that wall, there was Max out in the street barking at a mother and a child that just happened to be walking along there.

Of course, María started shouting, "Come here, Max. What are you doing out here? You're going to get run over. Bad dog. Why did you leave me?" And she grabbed him and took him back to Jeanette's house.

What had just happened? María said when she went out to get cuttings of the plants, Max wanted to go out with her. She took him out on a leash. However, after a while Max seemed anxious, so María took the leash off, giving him the command to stay right by her. Usually, he did stay by her. Then, she got so engrossed in looking for just the right places on the right plants to make the cuttings that she wasn't paying attention to what Max was doing. Luckily, I heard him.

Here was another "God moment." It really wasn't luck. I have no doubt that God had something to do with my timing to go outside. Then, God was there for Max, as those people were in the street just at that moment, resulting in Max barking up a storm so I could hear him. Had it not been for those people, Max might have continued running in that street and could have been run over. People who travel that road drive quite fast and wouldn't be expecting a cute little dog to be running around loose. And if he hadn't been run over, he could've gotten lost. Max doesn't know his way around where Jeanette lives like he does around my neighborhood and María's neighborhood. Also, God was with that mother and child, as Max didn't attack them. His bark is worse than his bite.

Losing Max would have been a tremendous tragedy. He is like my daughter María's child. Her dogs are her everything, as her son lives in Maryland, and her dogs are her company, her life. María and I were both so emotionally affected by all this that we could hardly think of anything else. The whole ride back home we kept saying, "Thank the Lord. Thank the Lord that nothing happened to Max, and he's here safe with us." That night I kept saying, "Thank you, thank you, thank you, God!" all night long.

And Max will always be on a leash from now on.

Lesson learned: Don't count on your pet staying next to you without a leash on. There are too many distractions, and bad things could happen.

My Lucky Day

or

More of God's Blessings

"I'm going to pay for your lunch today—and the yearly dues." That was my good friend Yvette. Today was the April luncheon of the El Paso Retired Teachers Association. We look forward to that, as it's a fun time to get together, chat with other retired teachers, listen to a guest speaker, and eat a delicious meal. We both had just started to attend these meetings, and we find them entertaining.

Well, that was just super. Yvette is sweet like that. She also brought a bag of books to donate for the book table. We retired teachers are urged to bring in books, movies, and CDs to share with each other. Any of the above that remain at the end of our meeting are donated to various other organizations. Craft materials are also greatly appreciated. They are taken to various schools and daycare centers for the children.

Well, my luck continued on this day. A lady named Pat called out, "Is the lady that wanted *Chicken Soup for the Soul* books here? I brought her a lot more." I immediately raised my hand high. She came over to me and told me she had brought me several bags of those books in case I wanted them. They were in her trunk, and I could go get them with her after the meeting. Last month she had set **seven books** from that series on the book table. I took all seven. I was really looking for the book *Chicken Soup for the Preteen Soul* at that time to give to my granddaughter when I went to visit her in Phoenix. That one was not included in the set, but I was very happy to get the other books that month, and again this month. This time she had brought me **fifteen more books** of that series. She said a friend of hers had given them to her, and she was done with them. She had considered setting them out on her sidewalk for people to take as they wished but then remembered the book table. Well, I told her she had made my day. Imagine that. Twenty-two books from the *Chicken Soup for the Soul* series. There are a couple of books destined for nurses. I know just who I am going to pass those along to. There are books about pets, miracles, encouragement for divorced people, married people, parents—just about anyone you could think of. I read the *Chicken Soup for the Preteen Soul* while I was visiting my granddaughter. (I did buy that one.) I would recommend it as a gift for any preteen. It is full of stories that that age level can relate to dealing with making good choices, helping others, getting along, preteen problems, encouragement, and so much more.

I knew about these books, as I had used some of the short stories from one of them to illustrate what I was teaching my ESOL students during various modules at school, and also as fillers for encouragement when teaching "bell to bell."

My luck didn't end there. The luncheon always has a raffle to earn more money for the projects taken on. People bring in something they want to regift or just donate. They put their items in gift bags and place them on the designated table. Anybody who wants to can buy raffle tickets, and the items are raffled off. Well, as luck would have it, my number was called out first, so I chose the El Paso Retired Teachers Free Luncheon Certificate—a $25 value. How about that?

Are you ready for more? Yes, my luck continued. After the luncheon, I went to Sam's Club to pick up a few things. I saw the most beautiful *"lengua de suegra"* plant, or snake plant. (Haha. "Lengua de suegra" means "mother-in-law's tongue". Not a very nice name for this plant. Whoever named it in Spanish sure didn't like his/her mother-in-law.) Anyway, I figured I'd break down and buy it. I also found a pair of capris pants I liked. Then, I looked for the items I needed at that time. When I got to the register, the attendant asked me if I wanted to use my points.

"I have points?" I asked. She answered that I had $193. My bill was for $123. I said, "Sure!" I was as happy as a lark.

I was so excited with all these blessings that when my daughter came to visit so we could walk her dogs, I told her all about my day. I told her I got the capris pants I was wearing. She asked me, "How much were they?" I laughed cheerfully and exclaimed, "They were FREE!"

We had a hearty laugh after that. Then I suggested that we should go buy a couple of scratch-off lottery tickets. If I ever was going to win, this could be my day. Well, we did, and I didn't. Haha. I think God was telling me enough was enough. My friend Yvette responded when I told her about the lottery tickets that that was okay, I had had a good run. I must agree. It was a super day.

Observation: Unexpected kindnesses, no matter how big or how small, can really make a difference to the receiving person.

Humble yourselves therefore under the mighty hand of God, that he may exalt you in due time.

1 Peter 5:6

CHAPTER TWENTY-EIGHT
Travel Delights and Travel Plights

What's a great way to create memories for yourself and your family? Travel. There are so many benefits of travel. Travel can broaden our minds, increase our understanding of other cultures, of people's different cuisines, of different ways of thinking, and even speaking. Travel makes life more interesting, and it's a fantastic way to create a stronger bond with loved ones. It's a creative way to forget about—or at least minimize—our problems and frustrations, and to get a new perspective on life. And travel allows us to truly appreciate the beauty and diversity of God's creation. Need a break from work or monotony? Feeling adventurous? Try zip-lining through a forest or over a lake. Rent a pontoon boat or a speed boat or tour on one. Take a hike through a canyon or up into the mountains. Swim in the ocean (watch out for the sharks) or find an over-the-water rope tree and do a rope swing into an inviting body of water (but be careful—this could be dangerous). Curious about exotic foods? Try some spicy Indian food or some scrumptious chiles en nogada, or Greek moussaka, lamb gyros full of tzatziki, and baklava for the finishing touch. Or buy one of those coveted turkey legs from a food truck or at a fair. There's food for everyone's palate, and it's such a delight to sample exotic—or at least somewhat different—foods. My family and I have done all the above and have fantastic memories as a by-product. Such memories are a great way to leave a legacy for loved ones.

I have always loved to travel. My parents took my brother, sister, and me all around the United States as we were growing up. I have so many precious memories of those times. And my travels have continued ever since. And my daughters and grandchildren share this love of travel with me. Many of our favorite, greatest pleasures have come from our special trips. God has been good to us and has made this all possible.

Two special trips we take each year are types of family reunions. One of these is our annual trip up into the majestic mountains of Ruidoso, New Mexico, about a three-hour drive from El Paso. We have been having these family reunions in Ruidoso since 1984, when I invested in a timeshare as a way to repay my parents for always taking my daughters and me in every summer when we would visit them while we lived in Mexico. My daughters and I accompanied my parents up to Ruidoso that year because Mom and Dad had received an invitation to check out a timeshare property that was being built there and were offered a free grandfather clock for the visit. My dad was always for getting bargains—and free is the best (I follow in his footsteps there), so off we all went. Well, while my daughters went off exploring the property, I sat in on the spiel with my parents—and I was the one who ended up buying the timeshare (and getting the free grandfather clock, which I took all the way down to Mexico). And I've never been sorry.

Before that, every summer, my daughters and I would go up to El Paso from Tuxtla Gutierrez and stay the summers. I would continue my education at the University of Texas at El Paso. My mom worked in the Humanities department as the senior secretary for Dr. Diana Natalicio, who later became president of that university. I would ride back and forth with Mom to the campus and then go to summer school classes in the mornings to finish my bachelor's degree and my master's degree. I'd meet Mom at noon to go out to lunch together. Then, I'd stay in the Humanities building and study until she was ready to drive back home. I put my young daughters in Kinder Care and the YWCA while we were doing that. My daughters benefited greatly, as they learned the songs, games, and activities of American children there while they improved their acquisition of the English language. Mom and I would pick them up on the way back from UTEP, and, when we'd get back, we'd wait for Dad to come home so we could all eat and be together. We loved to play games then. One of our favorites was this great game of Memory that had an enormous number of cards. They would cover the whole table when they were spread out. Well, it seemed like every time it was my dad's turn to uncover two cards to try to make a match, he'd uncover the same cards. I don't know if he did that on purpose or not, but my kids would get quite a kick out of it. They still mention that to this day.

Dad and Mom loved to take us on a trip each summer when we visited them. Well, from 1984 on, each summer we went up into those gorgeous mountains and the cool fresh air in Ruidoso for an exciting week at the timeshare resort. My week is the Fourth of July week, so we would always go—and still go—to The Flying J Ranch for their barbecue and show, the famous Fourth of July fireworks over the lake at the Inn of the Mountain Gods, shopping in the quaint village of Ruidoso, betting on horses at the races at Ruidoso Downs, horseback riding among the trees, exploring nearby towns and attractions, and so much more. And it is always such a treat just to stand on our balcony and look out over the virgin forest and enjoy the magnificent view, God's masterpiece. My daughters started going there when they were young. We were three generations. Then, my daughters had their own children, and we all continued going every Fourth of July week. That was then four generations. My parents have gone on to be with their Lord, but we are still three generations enjoying this amazing time all together up in Ruidoso. It's an added blessing that we can escape from the sweltering El Paso and Phoenix summers for that week.

We all have such fantastic memories of these years up in Ruidoso. And we always plan our summers around that week to make sure that we can continue to unite up there. It is so import- ant to me to foster these memories, these get-togethers. I consider this part of my legacy, and I hope my children and grandchildren con- tinue this tradition after I'm gone. Which reminds me, that is where I want my ashes to be scattered when I die (if it's not against the  law)—NOT planted under a tree or a bush, as it would be terrible if that tree or bush would then die. I want my family to stand on the upstairs balcony of our unit and scatter the ashes to the winds during a gorgeous sunset. What a superb way to reunite with my Lord.

The second annual trip we try to make together is a week at Los Abrigados Resort in Sedona, Arizona. This trip doesn't have a set date like our week in Ruidoso. We plan it for whenever we can all, or almost all, make it. This we have been doing ever since my youngest daughter got married there in the most beautiful wedding set up right on the resort's riverbank. We all fell in love with the area. The resort has so much to offer, as does the area: the beguiling red rock formations, the challenging hiking trails, the gurgling, refreshing rivers, the archaeo- logical sites, and so much more.

Besides these family reunions, I take awesome fall break trips to a variety of places on the East Coast and the West Coast, and in between with my youngest daughter, Ana, and her daughter, Lily. I take fun trips also with my daughters Maria Fernanda and Jeanette and their children to go visit Cat and Lily in Phoenix or to travel with any combination of children and grandchildren around the country—to California, the ocean, tourist attractions, visit my brother's family, to Florida for more tourist attractions, and to visit my daughters' Tío Agustin: all directions, always exploring, always discovering exciting places, and foods, and creating meaningful experiences with each other.

Yes, God has been good to us and has enabled us to take these vacations together, and we are extremely thankful to Him for these opportunities. Hopefully, you can create meaningful familial bonds—and a lasting legacy—experiencing travel in your own ways, too.

Along with travel delights can come travel mishaps. I have had some interesting moments. One was when my daughters María and Ana and I were taking German classes in the evenings at Cosmolingua School in Tuxtla Gutierrez with Martin Dettmer, a German friend of ours. As a culmination of the course, our class took a trip with Martin around some areas of Chiapas in a tour bus to practice our German. I don't know how much German we spoke, but I do know we had a lot of fun. There was just one problem. When we got out of the bus near the famous *cascadas* (waterfalls) of Agua Azul and commenced exploring the area, I slipped in one of the pools of water and sprained my ankle badly. That made the rest of the trip quite challenging, as I could hardly walk.

A silly mishap occurred during one of the times I took students to Washington, D.C. for the Close Up for New Americans program. We were walking down the sidewalk in the direction of the National Holocaust Museum to get entrance tickets. I was talking to my friend and fellow sponsor Lucy when, suddenly, I was much, much shorter than she was. What had just happened? Well, I was talking to her and not paying attention to where I was walking, and I walked right into about two feet of wet cement some men had just placed in a hole they had dug around a tree there. I'll never forget the look of horror on her face. I found out later that she was afraid I was going to belt out a number of expletives after that happened. But that's not me. I just started laughing hysterically. And then we continued on to our destination to get our tickets. While we were waiting in line, some of my students took turns trying to hit the cement off of my pants leg with one of the guy's bandanas. We got our timed tickets and continued sightseeing. As I kept walking, little bits of cement would fly into the air. (They were bell bottom pants, so the material was flexible.) By the end of the day, all the cement had left my pants. That happened to be the year I was able to take my daughter Ana with me to experience the program. I guess she must have been embarrassed—I'm not sure if for her or for me. When we got back to El Paso, Ana shared that story with her sisters Jeanette and María, and they all remembered a similar incident when they were little and we were sightseeing in downtown Oaxaca, Mexico, with their dad. All of a sudden, I was almost as short as they were. Again, I obviously was not paying attention, and I stepped into a hole just like the hole of the wet cement—minus the cement, though. I had been wearing a dress with a very billowy skirt, and, as I stepped into the hole, the skirt opened up, and it looked like I was wearing an umbrella. Goodness gracious.

During one of our family reunions to Sedona, Arizona, María, her sons, and I went to Slide Rock outside of the city. It is appropriately named, as the area has red-rock "slides" that water flows down. People can swim and slide at their own risk. Well, we were there a little while when my daughter and her sons decided they wanted to go farther into the wooded area behind the slide area to explore. I didn't want to go with them, as I didn't know what kind of terrain there would be, so I stayed with our gear. They were gone for a while, and I decided I was going to get up and try to walk on the wet rock. Big mistake. No sooner had I taken a few steps and, BONK. I took a nasty fall. It was so hard that someone from across the slide area heard my head hit the rock and came *rushing* as fast as possible careful not to fall himself, to check if I was okay. I am totally convinced God was with me that time. I could have easily died. I stayed sitting up on the side of the "slides" until my family came back, at which time I told them what had happened. I thank the Lord everything turned out okay. (Do you see a pattern emerging when I don't pay attention?)

Now to a different kind of problem. What would you do if you were on a trip in a foreign country with family members and you got separated from them and you couldn't communicate with them? That happened in 2011 when I went on an amazing trip with my daughter María and my grandsons Luis and Cris. We flew to Burlington, Vermont, and ate at Shanty on the Shore. From there we drove in a rental car to the Smugglers' Notch Resort in the lush Green Mountains of Vermont. We enjoyed all the activities at the resort and traveled around the area marveling at the waterfalls and greenery everywhere, and the quaint mailboxes in the forms of trucks, horses, cows, pigs, and other unique shapes. We toured the original Ben and Jerry's factory and encountered, by chance, the Von Trapp Family Lodge—the place they settled in after fleeing Germany. My grandsons certainly enjoyed that, as one of their favorite movies is *The Sound of Music*. Then we proceeded to drive up into Canada and visit Montreal. We were awed by the beauty of the Basilique-Cathédrale Marie-Reine-du-Monde, the Notre-Dame Basilica, St. Patrick's Basilica, and other churches there. We shopped in the downtown area, went down to the harbor, and then we went to enter Chinatown through their traditional style Chinese arches to check out some of their Chinese sculptures and other tourist attractions. I guess I wasn't paying attention and got separated from them. The worst part was our phones didn't work there in Canada. What was I going to do? Were they missing me? How was I going to find them? I tried calling my daughter, but to no avail. Then I tried calling who I thought was my grandson Luis. Well, his father, also Luis, in El Paso answered. I was surprised. So was he. I had marked the wrong Luis in my phone contacts. Soon after, my daughter and grandsons retraced their steps and found me. Was I ever thankful to God that time. And we had another story to tell when we got back to El Paso.

In 2015, I took my daughter Maria and my grandsons Luis and Cris on a graduation trip for them to Italy and Greece. That trip was unforgettable in so many ways. It really opened my grandsons' eyes to the breathtaking marvels of the "Old World," the completely different architecture, foods, people, landscapes, and history. We threw coins into the Trevi Fountain in Rome, took a boat ride around the island of Capri, the boys swam in the Mediterranean Sea by our hotel in Sorrento, and we walked the still existing Roman streets of Pompeii. We also took a night ferry to Greece, explored the ruins and danced in a discotheque in Delphi; we climbed the rock stairs to explore the Acropolis in Athens, and visited many other landmarks there. But what part of this trip is mentioned the most? Well, when we were in the El Paso airport waiting for our plane to Italy, I thought I heard that our flight was boarding. I gathered my stuff and started walking down the tunnel to what I thought was our plane. (I don't know how the attendant allowed me to go there without the correct ticket.) My daughter and grandsons didn't follow me. They knew I had made a mistake and gone down the tunnel to the wrong plane. It didn't take me long to realize what I had done, and I started to go back. Meanwhile, my family had told the attendant what I had done. The attendant started asking, "Where's Grannie? Where's Grannie?" I think she was imagining a very stereotypical old grannie. Well, out I stepped from the tunnel—a rather young, agile, energetic "grannie". That question of, "Where's Grannie?" comes up jokingly too often.

Even with these—and probably other—mishaps, we really enjoy traveling. I wanted to include all these moments, the travel delights and the travel plights, in this memoir because they are part of the legacy I am leaving for my family. I want them to remember these special moments and continue to enjoy traveling together—even when I'm gone. I thought you may also enjoy these silly stories. I thank God for all these opportunities to travel together through the three and four generations. I know not everyone can have the same opportunities to travel, but we can all look for opportunities to bond with family members and leave a family legacy.

CHAPTER TWENTY-NINE

A Teacher's Legacy

or

Life in God's Service

As every man hath received the gift, even so minister the same one to another, as good stewards of the manifold grace of God.

1 Peter 4:10

Jesus was the ultimate teacher. His moral and spiritual teachings on unconditional love, forgiveness, and compassion form the foundation of Christianity and moral standards for people all around the world. God's emphasis on the importance of loving others is evident in His commandment, "Thou shalt love thy neighbor as thyself." (Matthew 22:39) The phrase in The Lord's Prayer, "Forgive us our sins; for we also forgive every one that is indebted to us," (Luke 11:4) teaches us the value of forgiveness. Jesus often stressed the importance of having compassion for all people, regardless of their social status or background. ("Judge not according to appearance, but judge righteous judgment." (John 7:24) He also had a suggested reaction to bullies: "Bless them that curse you, and pray for them which despitefully use you." (Luke

6:28) We may not be able to change those bullies, but we can change our response to them. Jesus showed that true greatness comes from serving others, as witnessed in His washing of His disciples' feet (John 13:1-5), and that we are to be humble, as we see Him being humble (Romans 12:16) and obedient even to the end as He was with His death on the cross. And then there are the many parables Jesus told to make His intended lessons understandable to His listeners. His legacy lives on to this day as a formidable teacher.

We are told to use whatever gift we have received to serve others, as faithful stewards of God's Grace. The whole chapter twelve of the book of Romans tells us how we should live and how we should serve others. The gift God gave me is the aptitude to teach and influence others in positive ways. I am in no way comparing myself to God/Jesus. I am just thanking Him for giving me this ability, as I truly enjoy teaching.

My brother always said he could be a professional student. I also love the educational environment. However, I am always a teacher of some sort, although I have also learned from my students. I have taught my daughters many things on an academic level and on a spiritual level, and now they are teaching their children. I taught English to girlfriends of mine in my house in Tuxtla. I have also taught many students throughout my fifteen years of teaching at the Universidad Autónoma de Chiapas and the Instituto Bicultural in Tuxtla Gutierrez, and my twenty-nine years at Burges High School in El Paso, Texas. Besides teaching my daughters English and Spanish, my elementary and middle school students English, social studies, Spanish, and music, and my high school and university students English, and English as a Second Language, I know I have influenced all these people in so many other ways as well. How have I influenced my family and students? I let my enthusiasm and love of learning show through. That enthusiasm is then replicated with my students. I respect my students, and my students have always respected me. I have inculcated in them respect for God, family, government, different cultures, different lifestyles, different ideas, and different places. With respect comes acceptance of others, and I have always encouraged everyone not to judge others, but rather to be patient, kind, and encouraging.

When I was teaching (I am now retired), I did all I could to make my classes exciting so my students would remember what they had learned. I made every effort to create interesting projects and inspiring lessons to motivate my students to do their best, set goals, and be successful.

"How do you get all your students in your classes to sing?" This was a question I would often get referring to my high school students. It took a bit of doing, but later they could be heard all the way down the hall as they sang with gusto.

"Ms. Sanchez, I was just in a grocery store, and over the intercom they were playing the song 'You've Got a Friend,' and I thought of you and your classes where we would sing those songs." That was Julio, a student I had had years before but whose memory was triggered by listening to that song. I get a lot of feedback from prior students about how they enjoyed my classes and were adept at speaking English partly because of my classes. (I can't take all the credit. Haha!) And I really appreciate Facebook, as it has enabled me to keep in touch with many of my students. I wish I knew how to contact more of them to see what they were up to now.

Travel was definitely a way to encourage students. I was the department chair for the ESOL program at Burges High School, and I was the sponsor of the Close Up for New Americans program there for twenty-four years. If you are a middle school or high school teacher and teach English or social studies, this program could be for you. You could be a sponsor for this at your school if there isn't a program established there already. Or, if you are reading this and have a son or daughter or grandchild in middle school or high school, this program could be for him or her if there is a Close Up program established at that school. If not, it could be a good time to suggest the school open up such a program for the students. There is a Close Up for New Americans program and a Close Up Program for American students. I opened my Close Up for New Americans programs to any ESOL student interested in participating in community service, representing the Close Up Club in school spirit activities, helping with fundraising, and participating in the national Close Up for New Americans program. This entails a week-long stay in Washington, D.C., to attend workshops, lectures by prominent Americans, field trips, and visits and study sessions about the national monuments, to learn about and then visit the Supreme Court, the House of Representatives and the Senate, and so much more. Students learn about the United States government by experiencing it. Often, I would be told, "Now, I understand what I was studying in my US History class!" This program also enables the formation of life-long relationships of participating students with students from other places in the United States. The added bonus for our program is that the "New Americans" were from all over the world, so my students were enthused to learn about the cultures of their respective countries.

The Close Up for New Americans program was the perfect program for ESOL students who didn't think they fit in other clubs because of their limited proficiency in English or any other reason. They felt comfortable with the ESOL students in the program and with me. They did have to become extroverts to do the necessary fundraising to earn their part of the program's cost. (The district provided some money for them.) Soon the participants were selling posters, candy, and whatever they could to earn money. We had carwashes until the district forbade them. The students wrote letters to local companies requesting donations. All these activities gave them opportunities for social growth as well as academic growth.

Another goal I had for the students of the Close Up for New Americans program was to get them active in community service. I opened this up to other students of mine, also, if they were interested. The students volunteered to paint houses for Project Bravo and Christmas in April. They also volunteered at the Child Crisis Center and played Bingo with the residents of an old folks' home behind Burges. It was so wonderful to see how proud these students were of being able to help others. And they learned how to paint and do other home projects at the same time. Everything associated with these students' participation in the Close Up programs helped them feel more fulfilled, and more capable.

Participation in the Close Up for New Americans program also gave these students a love for travel. I let my love of travel shine through, and it was contagious. The next step I wanted to take was to travel to Europe. Predicament: How does a single person on a teacher's salary travel the world? (Texas teachers did not make then what they make now.) Well, she takes her students with her. I had traveled extensively in Mexico and the United States, and a little in Canada. My daughters were grown, and I wanted to travel to Europe. In 2004, Chris B., a teacher friend of mine, was organizing a wonderful trip to Europe for interested students and adults. My daughter Ana was living and working in Houston at that time. She and I joined the group and had an exciting time traveling nine days through London, Stonehenge, Bath, and then Paris via the train under the English Channel. The trip was a traveler's dream.

Cris decided not to organize any more trips, but four years later another teacher who had taken the same trip to Europe with us asked me if I would like to organize a trip with her. That seemed perfect. I wasn't ready to be responsible for a whole group on my own yet, but I was definitely game for cosponsoring something. We took our five-day EF Tours Orientation Training in the fall of 2008 in Rome—sponsored by the company. We chose our trip, opened it up to students and adults, and started having meetings. Luckily, Elsa T., the teacher I was going to work with, was a whiz at computers and could take care of the PowerPoint presentations and technical aspects of the trip. Back then, I wasn't as technologically savvy. We worked hard to get that trip off the ground. I asked you earlier, "How does a single person on a teacher's salary travel the world?" Well, if you are willing to do the work, you can travel free. You need to have at least six paying travelers to go free when you sponsor the trip. (We used the company EF Tours.) We ended up with twenty-two travelers. It was a lot of work to get everything right for the trip and the travelers, but it was worth it. Spring Break of 2009, we embarked on our travels through Italy, visiting many important spots in Rome, Florence, Assisi, and Pisa. Another exciting trip for all participants. Elsa left our city to teach elsewhere, but almost every year after that first trip we cosponsored until 2019, I organized European trips for students and adults. What a thrill to see the wonder in everyone's eyes as they marveled at the famous landmarks, lay on the floor of the Tate Museum in London admiring their reflections on the ceiling, devoured a variety of authentic meals, traveled the country sides, swam in the Mediterranean Sea, visited a national stud farm in Kildare, Ireland (what dedication caring for those valuable horses), got the "Gift of Speech" as they hung upside down from the top of Blarney Castle (definitely the scariest activity I ever did), meandered through the open market corridors in Morocco savoring the numerous varieties of olives, shopped in the stores on the Ponte Vecchio in Florence, admired the statues of David, Medusa, and others on the main square there, and so much more. Lives were changed for the students and adults—and for me. Our memories of such unique adventures will be cherished for the rest of our lives.

Teaching is such a gratifying career—and there are exciting opportunities for teachers who are willing to search for them. I thank God for having bestowed this gift on me.

And we know that all things work together for good to them that love God, to them who are the called according to his purpose.

Romans 8:28

CHAPTER THIRTY

Final Chapter

To leave the world a bit better, whether by a healthy child, a garden patch, or a redeemed social condition; To know even one life has breathed easier because you have lived. This is to have succeeded.

From Ralph Waldo Emerson's poem "Success"

These are my family's stories about faith and family. They comprise our journey in two different places—the United States and Mexico. There are stories of times of great joy, times when life was tough, times when we laughed, and times when we cried, but through it all, we held on to our faith. The multiple purposes through these stories are to glorify God, to share my faith and show how it impacted my decisions, to leave a legacy for my family through their family history, and to invite you to reflect on the legacy you would like to leave behind for your loved ones. Living a meaningful life makes for a lasting legacy. We can think about ways we can make a difference beyond our lifetime. This is just the beginning. We can envision a future where our legacy continues to evolve. This is an invitation to embrace the values of faith, love, and the enduring strength of family bonds. We can use these gifts God gave us to help change the world. This book is not just about the past. It is also about the future—a future where legacy continues to unfold.

My darling daughters and my good-hearted grandchildren: A family is a gift to be nurtured and cherished. Regardless of the challenges life presents, the threads of faith, family, and love will guide you through it all. We are never alone. God is always with us, our constant companion, guiding us in this incredible journey called life. Give God all the credit. Give God all the glory. You have given me so much happiness. You have made me so proud. I have attempted to give you an understanding of your roots, your family history—where you came from and what has helped make you, <u>you</u>. I have recorded here vignettes of our lives and the lessons learned. We can see the presence of God at every step. God/Jesus protects us. He comforts us. He corrects us. He motivates us, and, ultimately, He will save us. God is our moral compass, our anchor. The most important thing I can leave you is faith: faith in God and faith in yourselves through our God.

Don't feel emptiness or despair.

What has gotten me through the dark times, the challenging times? The power of faith and family and knowing that God is in charge. How are we to react to what happens to us—and the world, for that matter?

When we are experiencing setbacks, and problems, we must be strong and stay anchored in our faith, unlike Peter, who, in the middle of the storm, walked on water until he took his eyes off Jesus and focused on the storm and became scared, thus falling into the water. We must keep our eyes on the Lord when we encounter adversity and suffering, and He will stretch His hands out to us, just as He did to Peter after he put his eyes back on Jesus. (Matthew 14:25-31) There will always be storms. We need to stay anchored in our Lord God.

We can ponder all of Jesus's earthly hardships and suffering, culminating with the excruciating pain he felt while being tortured and, ultimately, with His agonizing death on the cross. However, He overcame death and rose again, thus saving us from eternal suffering. God was with Him, and God is with us, too, through our pain and suffering, and we can look forward to joining Him one day in Paradise.

As for my legacy: Will the world be a better place because I existed? Have I made a difference? I certainly hope so. What do I want my legacy to be? What would be the happy ending to my story? To be a source of pride, motivation, and inspiration for others. To serve as a positive example for future generations. To pass on the values of faith, love, respect, compassion, and patience. To make a favorable impact on the lives of others.

To parents everywhere who want to do what's best for your children: Faith is the anchor. Family is love, support, and belonging. Communication is key. Building a family legacy can provide a purpose and manner to positively impact present and future generations.

CHAPTER THIRTY-ONE

God Is...
Bible Verse Chapter

We need to buy a lottery ticket to win.

We need to study the word of God to understand Him. The Bible is God's message to us written by men He inspired to provide us with a firm foundation in His teachings. I include here Bible verses I find comforting and inspiring, verses of messages about life, relationships, love, hope, and faith. I hope you find them comforting and inspiring, too.

Why study the Word of God?

2 Timothy 3:15-17 and how from infancy you have known the Holy Scriptures, which are able to make you wise for salvation through faith in Christ Jesus. All Scripture is God-breathed and is useful for teaching, rebuking, correcting and training in righteousness, so that the servant of God may be thoroughly equipped for every good work. (Paul's message in his letter to Timothy)

Joshua 1:8-9 This book of the law shall not depart out of thy mouth; but thou shalt meditate therein day and night, that thou mayest observe to do according to all that is written therein: for then thou shalt make thy way prosperous, and then thou shalt have good success. Have not I commanded thee? Be strong and of a good courage; be not afraid, neither be thou dismayed: for the Lord thy God is with thee whithersoever thou goest.

Romans 15:4 For whatsoever things were written aforetime were written for our learning, that we through patience and comfort of the scriptures might have hope.

Psalm 119:105 Thy word is a lamp unto my feet, and a light unto my path.

God is my father, my moral compass, the good shepherd. He motivates me. He comforts me. He corrects me.

Romans 8:14-17 For as many as are led by the Spirit of God, they are the sons of God. For ye have not received the spirit of bondage again to fear; but ye have received the Spirit of adoption, whereby we cry, Abba, Father. The Spirit itself beareth witness with our spirit, that we are the children of God: And if children, then heirs; heirs of God, and joint-heirs with Christ; if so be that we suffer with him, that we may be also glorified together.

Galatians 3:26 For ye are all the children of God by faith in Christ Jesus.

2 Corinthians 6:18 "I will be a Father to you, and you will be my sons and daughters, says the Lord Almighty."

Ephesians 5:1 Be ye therefore followers of God, as dear children; And walk in love, as Christ also hath loved us, and hath given himself for us an offering and a sacrifice to God for a sweetsmelling savour.

Revelation 3:19-21 As many as I love, I rebuke and chasten: be zealous therefore, and repent. Behold, I stand at the door, and knock: if any man hear my voice, and open the door, I will come in to him, and will sup with him, and he with me. To him that overcometh will I grant to sit with me in my throne, even as I also overcame, and am set down with my Father in his throne.

Proverbs 13:24 He that spareth his rod hateth his son: but he that loveth him chasteneth him betimes.

Proverbs 3:12 For whom the Lord loveth he correcteth; even as a father the son in whom he delighteth.

Psalm 118:17-19 I shall not die, but live, and declare the works of the Lord. The Lord hath chastened me sore: but he hath not given me over unto death. Open to me the gates of righteousness: I will go into them, and I will praise the Lord:

Hebrews 12:5-11 And ye have forgotten the exhortation which speaketh unto you as unto children, My son, despise not thou the chastening of the Lord, nor faint when thou art rebuked of him: For whom the Lord loveth he chasteneth, and scourgeth every son whom he receiveth. If ye endure chastening, God dealeth with you as with sons; for what son is he whom the father chasteneth not? But if ye be without chastisement, whereof all are partakers, then are ye bastards, and not sons. Furthermore we have had fathers of our flesh which corrected us, and we gave them reverence: shall we not much rather be in subjection unto the Father of spirits, and live? For they verily for a few days chastened us after their own pleasure; but he for our profit, that we might be partakers of his holiness. Now no chastening for the present seemeth to be joyous, but grievous: nevertheless afterward it yieldeth the peaceable fruit of righteousness unto them which are exercised thereby.

Psalm 119:67-77 Before I was afflicted I went astray: but now have I kept thy word. Thou art good, and doest good; teach me thy statutes. The proud have forged a lie against me: but I will keep thy precepts with my whole heart. Their heart is as fat as grease; but I delight in thy law. It is good for me that I have been afflicted; that I might learn thy statutes. The law of thy mouth is better unto me than thousands of gold and silver. Thy hands have made me and fashioned me: give me understanding, that I may learn thy commandments. They that fear thee will be glad when they see me; because I have hoped in thy word. I know, O Lord, that thy judgments are right, and that thou in faithfulness hast afflicted me. Let, I pray thee, thy merciful kindness be for my comfort, according to thy word unto thy servant. Let thy tender mercies come unto me, that I may live: for thy law is my delight.

Isaiah 64:8 But now, O Lord, thou art our father; we are the clay, and thou our potter; and we all are the work of thy hand.

Matthew 6:25-34 Therefore I say unto you, Take no thought for your life, what ye shall eat, or what ye shall drink; nor yet for your body, what ye shall put on. Is not the life more than meat, and the body than raiment? Behold the fowls of the air: for they sow not, neither do they reap, nor gather into barns; yet your heavenly Father feedeth them. Are ye not much better than they? Which of you by taking thought can add one cubit unto his stature? And why take ye thought for raiment? Consider the lilies of the field, how they grow; they toil not, neither do they spin: And yet I say unto you, That even Solomon in all his glory was not arrayed like one of these. Wherefore, if God so clothe

the grass of the field, which to day is, and to morrow is cast into the oven, shall he not much more clothe you, O ye of little faith?

Therefore take no thought, saying, What shall we eat? or, What shall we drink? or, Wherewithal shall we be clothed? (For after all these things do the Gentiles seek:) for your heavenly Father knoweth that ye have need of all these things. But seek ye first the kingdom of God, and his righteousness; and all these things shall be added unto you. Take therefore no thought for the morrow: for the morrow shall take thought for the things of itself. Sufficient unto the day is the evil thereof.

Luke 12:31-32 But rather seek ye the kingdom of God; and all these things shall be added unto you. Fear not, little flock; for it is your Father's good pleasure to give you the kingdom.

And so also should we as fathers and mothers be with our offspring: Deuteronomy 6:5-7 And thou shalt love the Lord thy God with all thine heart, and with all thy soul, and with all thy might. And these words, which I command thee this day, shall be in thine heart: And thou shalt teach them diligently unto thy children, and shalt talk of them when thou sittest in thine house, and when thou walkest by the way, and when thou liest down, and when thou risest up.

Psalm 103:17-18 But the mercy of the Lord is from everlasting to everlasting upon them that fear him, And his righteousness unto children's children; To such as keep his covenant, And to those that remember his commandments to do them.

God is love.
John 3:16 For God so loved the world, that he gave his only begotten Son, that whosoever believeth in him should not perish, but have

everlasting life. (The Bible in a nutshell.) There is no greater love.

Romans 8:2-4 There is therefore now no condemnation to them which are in Christ Jesus, who walk not after the flesh, but after the Spirit. For the law of the Spirit of life in Christ Jesus hath made me free from the law of sin and death. For what the law could not do, in that it was weak through the flesh, God sending his own Son in the likeness of sinful flesh, and for sin, condemned sin in the flesh: That the righteousness of the law might be fulfilled in us, who walk not after the flesh, but after the Spirit.

God is hope.
John 14:27 Peace I leave with you, my peace I give unto you: not as the world giveth, give I unto you. Let not your heart be troubled, neither let it be afraid.

Isaiah 40:31 But they that wait upon the Lord shall renew their strength; they shall mount up with wings as eagles; they shall run, and not be weary; and they shall walk, and not faint.

Deuteronomy 31:8 And the Lord, he it is that doth go before thee; he will be with thee, he will not fail thee, neither forsake thee: fear not, neither be dismayed.

1 Corinthians 10:13 There hath no temptation taken you but such as is common to man: but God is faithful, who will not suffer you to be tempted above that ye are able; but will with the temptation also make a way to escape, that ye may be able to bear it.

Philippians 4:6-7 Be careful for nothing; but in every thing by prayer and supplication with thanksgiving let your requests be made known unto God. And the peace of God, which passeth all understanding, shall keep your hearts and minds through Christ Jesus.

John 14:1-3 Let not your heart be troubled: ye believe in God, believe also in me. In my Father's house are many mansions: if it were not so, I would have told you. I go to prepare a place for you. And if I go and prepare a place for you, I will come again, and receive you unto myself; that where I am, there ye may be also.

John 14:18-21 I will not leave you comfortless: I will come to you. Yet a little while, and the world seeth me no more; but ye see me: because I live, ye shall live also. At that day ye shall know that I am in my Father, and ye in me, and I in you. He that hath my commandments, and keepeth them, he it is that loveth me: and he that loveth me shall be loved of my Father, and I will love him, and will manifest myself to him.

John 5:24 Verily, verily, I say unto you, He that heareth my word, and believeth on him that sent me, hath everlasting life, and shall not come into condemnation; but is passed from death unto life.

Romans 6:23 For the wages of sin is death; but the gift of God is eternal life through Jesus Christ our Lord.

Matthew 11:28 Come unto me, all ye that labour and are heavy laden, and I will give you rest.

Revelation 21:1-6 And I saw a new heaven and a new earth: for the first heaven and the first earth were passed away; and there was no more sea. And I John saw the holy city, new Jerusalem, coming down from God out of heaven, prepared as a bride adorned for her husband. And I heard a great voice out of heaven saying, Behold, the tabernacle of God is with men, and he will dwell with them, and they shall be his people, and God himself shall be with them, and be their God. And God shall wipe away all tears from their eyes; and there shall be no more death, neither sorrow, nor crying, neither shall there be any more pain: for the former things are passed away. And he that sat upon the throne said, Behold, I make all things new. And he said unto me, Write: for these words are true and faithful. And he said unto me, It is done. I am Alpha and Omega, the beginning and the end. I will give unto him that is athirst of the fountain of the water of life freely. He that overcometh shall inherit all things; and I will be his God, and he shall be my son.

God is a strong and trustworthy anchor for our souls. God is our anchor in the midst of life's stormy sea. He is the anchor that steadies our soul.

Hebrews 6:19 Which hope we have as an anchor of the soul, both sure and stedfast, and which entereth into that within the veil

God is our rock.
Psalm 62:6-7 He only is my rock and my salvation: he is my defence; I shall not be moved. In God is my salvation and my glory: the rock of my strength, and my refuge, is in God.

2 Samuel 22:32-34 For who is God, save the Lord? and who is a rock, save our God? God is my strength and power: and he maketh my way perfect. He maketh my feet like hinds' feet: and setteth me upon my high places.

Psalm 18:46 The Lord liveth; and blessed be my rock; and let the God of my salvation be exalted.

Psalms 62:7-8 In God is my salvation and my glory: the rock of my strength, and my refuge, is in God. Trust in him at all times; ye people, pour out your heart before him: God is a refuge for us.

Proverbs 30:5 Every word of God is pure: he is a shield unto them that put their trust in him.

Faith in God is our cornerstone, our foundation.
Isaiah 41:10 Fear thou not; for I am with thee: be not dismayed; for I am thy God: I will strengthen thee; yea, I will help thee; yea, I will uphold thee with the right hand of my righteousness.

Psalms 59:16 But I will sing of thy power; yea, I will sing aloud of thy mercy in the morning: for thou hast been my defence and refuge in the day of my trouble.

Foundations matter:
The parable of the wise and foolish builders:
Matthew 24-27 Therefore whosoever heareth these sayings of mine, and doeth them, I will liken him unto a wise man, which built his house upon a rock: And the rain descended, and the floods came, and the winds blew, and beat upon that house; and it fell not: for it was founded upon a rock. And every one that heareth these sayings of mine, and doeth them not, shall be likened unto a foolish man, which built his house upon the sand: And the rain descended, and the floods came, and the winds blew, and beat upon that house; and it fell: and great was the fall of it.

My God, my Jesus protects me. He is my savior.
Romans 5:19 For as by one man's disobedience many were made sinners, so by the obedience of one shall many be made righteous.

Isaiah 53:5 But he was wounded for our transgressions, he was bruised for our iniquities: the chastisement of our peace was upon him; and with his stripes we are healed.

Luke 12:8 Also I say unto you, Whosoever shall confess me before men, him shall the Son of man also confess before the angels of God.

Romans 8:2-4 Because through Christ Jesus the law of the Spirit who gives life has set you free from the law of sin and death. For what the law was powerless to do because it was weakened by the flesh, God did by sending his own Son in the likeness of sinful flesh to be a sin offering And so he condemned sin in the flesh, in order that the righteous requirement of the law might be fully met in us, who do not live according to the flesh but according to the Spirit.

Psalms 68:19-20 Blessed be the Lord, who daily loadeth us with benefits, even the God of our salvation. Selah. He that is our God is the God of salvation; and unto God the Lord belong the issues from death.

Romans 6:23 For the wages of sin is death; but the gift of God is eternal life through Jesus Christ our Lord.

Romans 10:9-10 That if thou shalt confess with thy mouth the Lord Jesus, and shalt believe in thine heart that God hath raised him from the dead, thou shalt be saved. For with the heart man believeth unto righteousness; and with the mouth confession is made unto salvation.

God is my protector.

Proverbs 30:5 Every word of God is pure: he is a shield unto them that put their trust in him.

Ephesians 6:10-11 [10] Finally, my brethren, be strong in the Lord, and in the power of his might. [11] Put on the whole armour of God, that ye may be able to stand against the wiles of the devil.

Psalm 29:11 The Lord will give strength unto his people; the Lord will bless his people with peace.

Psalm 34:17-19 The righteous cry, and the Lord heareth, and delivereth them out of all their troubles. The Lord is nigh unto them that are of a broken heart; and saveth such as be of a contrite spirit. Many are the afflictions of the righteous: but the Lord delivereth him out of them all.

Romans 8:31-39 What shall we then say to these things? If God be for us, who can be against us? He that spared not his own Son, but delivered him up for us all, how shall he not with him also freely give us all things? Who shall lay any thing to the charge of God's elect? It is God that justifieth. Who is he that condemneth? It is Christ that died, yea rather, that is risen again, who is even at the right hand of God, who also maketh intercession for us. Who shall separate us from the love of Christ? shall tribulation, or distress, or persecution, or famine, or nakedness, or peril, or sword? As it is written, For thy sake we are killed all the day long; we are accounted as sheep for the slaughter. Nay, in all these things we are more than conquerors through him that loved us. For I am persuaded, that neither death, nor life, nor angels, nor principalities, nor powers, nor things present, nor things to come,

Nor height, nor depth, nor any other creature, shall be able to separate us from the love of God, which is in Christ Jesus our Lord.

God has given us the power of faith. I know my God is with me always, and I know that I will be saved.

All Bible verses in this book are in the King James Version.

I Value Your Feedback

Thank you for reading *Faith, Family, and Memories: Stories of Our Lives in the United States, Mexico, and Back.* Your thoughts and feedback are incredibly important to me. I hope that our stories of faith, family, and resilience have touched your heart and inspired you in your own journey.

How to Leave a Review

If you are enjoying this book and find it meaningful, I would be grateful if you could take a moment to share your thoughts with others. Your review will help spread the message of faith and family to more readers.

Here are a couple of ways you can leave a review:

1. **Amazon**: Visit the book's page on Amazon and leave your review. Your insights will help potential readers understand what to expect and how the book can impact their lives.
2. **Goodreads**: If you're a member of Goodreads, please consider rating and reviewing the book there. Goodreads reviews are a great way to reach a community of avid readers.

What You Could Include in Your Review

When writing your review, consider including the following:

+ What story or message resonated with you the most?
+ How did the book impact your perspective on faith and family?
+ Did any particular chapters or anecdotes stand out to you?
+ Would you recommend this book to others? Why?

Thank you so much!

Call to Action Page

Discover Your Own Family History

Thank you for reading *Faith, Family, and Memories: Stories of Our Lives in the United States, Mexico, and Back.* I hope our journey has inspired you to explore and cherish your own family's history and stories.

As a special thank you, I would like to offer you a free PDF of the Family History Project I have developed. This project is designed to help you document and preserve your family's unique legacy for future generations.

Get Your Free Family History Project PDF.

Simply email your request to suew.sanchez@gmail.com
Your email will only be used to send you your PDF and occasional updates about my books.

Thank you for joining me in celebrating the importance of family and faith. I look forward to hearing about your own family history journey!

Connect With Me

I'd love to hear from you!